LIFE OR DEATH
LISTENING

A Hostage Negotiator's How-to Guide to
Mastering the Essential Communication Skill

Dan Oblinger

Kindle Direct Publishing

CONTENTS

Title Page

Copyright

Epigraph

Dedication

1. SIX STORIES UP   1

2. LIFE OR DEATH   6

3. MORE CAMPFIRES   9

4. RADICALLY SIMILAR   13

5. EXCELLENCE IN LISTENING   18

6. NOT LISTENING   23

7. THIS IS LISTENING   33

8. LEADERS WHO LISTEN   43

9. THE CULTURE BEAST   51

10. EMPATHY   56

11. RAPPORT   61

12. INFLUENCE   65

13. A PREFACE TO ALS   70

14. ASK BETTER QUESTIONS   73

15. REWARDING STORYTELLERS   81

16. TAMING EMOTIONS   86

17. SOMETIMES SAY NOTHING   92

18. POWERFUL WORDS 99

19. INSIGHTFUL LISTENING 103

20. THE RUN DOWN 107

21. SENDING THE MESSAGE 111

22. BUILDING A LISTENING CULTURE 115

23. THE HOMEFRONT 124

24. AN ENDING THAT IS A BEGINNING 128

QUICK REFERENCE 132

THE 8 ACTIVE LISTENING SKILLS 133

COMMONLY LABELED EMOTIONS 136

NOW WHAT? 137

About The Author 139

Books By This Author 141

"*I have discovered that most people have no one to talk to, no one, that is, who really wants to listen. When it does at last dawn on a man that you really want to hear about his business, the look that comes over his face is something to see.*"

—WALKER PERCY, THE MOVIEGOER

DEDICATION

To Christ, who is the very model of a leader who listens;

To My Le, my constant helpmate;

And to Police negotiators everywhere who answer the call and save lives through intentional listening.

1. SIX STORIES UP

a beginning

"At the intersection where your gifts, talents, and abilities meet a human need; therein you will discover your purpose."
—*Aristotle*

Y ou are driving down the street. All the concerns and worries of the day are on your mind. For the purposes of this thought experiment, it does not matter who you are, what you do, or what you know. As you drive, you see a group of people on the sidewalk pointing upwards. You stop your car. You get out. You look up. Six stories above the street, a young woman is dangling over the edge of a parking garage rooftop. As if possessed by an outside force, you run up the stairwell to the top floor. You find yourself standing face-to-face with this woman. She's going to jump! What do you do? What do you say?

Before I was a corporate trainer, author, keynote speaker, or a hostage negotiator, I was a beat cop in a large city in the middle of the United States. One fateful night as a young police officer driving a solo car, I was sent to the top of a six-story parking garage after a security officer found a woman trespassing on the roof.

That night, there was a brisk breeze. The "trespasser" was a young woman clinging to a guard rail with her feet dangling over the street below. I crept towards her until she told me she would jump if I came any closer. Then she said, "Do you believe in God?"

I ask you, dear reader, "What would you do?" It's not an academic scenario. It happened to me. If you have little experience with suicidal jumpers like I did so many years ago, you might be dumbfounded. How long can you talk to her? As a perfect stranger, can you convince her not to jump? What happens if you fail?

Lesson number one when intervening in crisis or conflict is to have courage. I commend all my audience members who would take a risk and engage in dialogue with my "jumper". It would be an easy option for many people to ignore this woman and her awkward, uncomfortable situation. I know because so many people I worked with as a police crisis negotiator had been ignored by so many people in their lives.

Now let us go back to that garage rooftop many years ago. Up to that point in my life, I had not given hostage negotiations or suicidal jumpers much thought. As a new police officer, I was woefully unprepared to help her. I was accustomed to giving orders and using reasonable force to back them up. I was in the habit of telling people what to do to solve my policing problems.

Today, as a corporate trainer and student of masterful listening, I often put my workshop attendees and keynote audiences in the shoes of that rookie cop. I ask them what they would do. The most common response is that they would talk to the troubled woman. Reason with her. Beg and plead her not to take her own life. The most common initial attempt to intervene is, "Don't do it!"

You want her to live. You know that suicide is a "permanent solution to a temporary problem". You know that her suicide would have a devastating impact on everyone she knows. It would impact the emergency workers who will deal with the aftermath. You know that there are robust systems of aid for the depressed and suicidal in many communities. You have 50 rational reasons you could give her not to jump. Unfortunately, rational people rarely find themselves on the wrong side of the guard rail on a six-story parking garage. None of that matters.

The first lesson I learned that night is the first one I would like to share with you as a reader of this book. It's not about you. If you mistakenly approach this listening opportunity thinking it's about you, you have set yourself up for failure. With a self-centered mindset, you will create anxiety and pressure for yourself by desperately searching for the one thing you have to say to save her. You'll dread saying the one thing that will make her jump. Both worries are well-intentioned. Both are irrelevant. Her decision to jump or live has little to do with your words. It has a lot more to do with whether she believes that you care. In the end, it's not about you. The decision is hers alone.

The first lesson I learned that night is the first one I would like to share with you as a reader of this book. It's not about you.

Now for another question. I'll ask you just as I ask my workshop participants, "How long can you make an appeal to a total stranger?" Most people are overly optimistic, particularly those who consider themselves "good talkers". In practice, I've found most people run out of good talking material for depressed and suicidal audiences after about 15 minutes. I know this well, because I ran out of material at about that point, too.

Once you realize it's not about you, a curious change occurs. My "Eureka!" moment only came when I ran out of words and emotional energy. Then, I quit trying to talk her into what I wanted. I started asking smart questions and listening to her answers. I was so exhausted that I had to let her carry the conversation. That's when I began to see positive change. Asking some simple questions might tell you why she is on the ledge. You might learn why she is on *this* ledge, why she is here *tonight*, what she is up against, and what she thinks she needs. These are essential bits of information that you'll never know if you just talk at her. Here's a lesson for leaders who must listen: it is nearly impossible to learn something new by speaking.

Here's a lesson for leaders who must listen: it is nearly impossible to learn something new by speaking.

The lessons I learned on that roof have stuck with me for life. The hardest lesson was to stop talking so much and start listening with intention. Once I did, my life changed forever. Despite my failings and my insufficient skill during my test on the parking garage roof, something great happened. I had found the intersection of my talents and a clear human need. That night, I resolved to become a hostage negotiator.

I studied. I practiced. I learned from experienced negotiators. Seven years later, I was selected in a competitive process for the position of hostage negotiator. Since then, I have completed the FBI National Crisis Negotiations Course. I have given and received specialized training in crisis negotiations to practitioners from Cape Cod to California. I have been the primary negotiator for jumpers, jilted teenaged lovers, veterans with PTSD, hostage takers, robbers, killers, and thieves. I've helped talk down drunks, drug addicts, and the mentally ill. I've bargained for time and lives. Through all these exotic situations, I have learned that success always comes back to basic listening skills and simple techniques to demonstrate empathy. These methods boil down to the first principle of listening: it's not about me.

I propose to give you a guided tour of listening and then show the specialized application of this skill to corporate leadership and caring for our loved ones. I believe that listening is the most important skill for achieving excellence in any human endeavor. There is no substitute. I believe that our communities, businesses, civic organizations, and families need better leaders and better lovers. We need master listeners! I hope this book helps you be just that. I hope the content in this modest book changes the trajectory of your personal and professional life forever for the good of all you meet. Let us begin.

2. LIFE OR DEATH

high-stakes listening

"When lives are at stake, leave nothing to chance."
—*Heckler & Koch GmbH marketing slogan, circa 1999*

W hen a hostage negotiator puts on his headset or walks to the edge of a rooftop to parlay with a jumper, the stakes are life-or-death. If a negotiator fails as a listener, someone may die. Whenever the SWAT page jolts me out of bed, I don my negotiator vest and know that I'm playing a potentially deadly game. When the police call the police because the situation is more than regular police officers can manage, the crisis is potentially lethal. I know this and accept it as a fact of my life. Truth be told, the high stakes of our calling motivate police crisis negotiators. Our job is the ultimate listening challenge.

Now let me show you the stakes for listening for everyone else. Picture your most important human relationship. In your mind, weigh the importance of this person in your life. Recall all the fond memories, admiration, and kindness he or she has given you. Think of the wonderful experiences and shared beliefs that created this trust you share! Now, like the Grinch, I'm going to steal something. I'm not taking away Christmas! Instead, I'll completely remove listening from your cherished relationship. You will never again listen to him or her. This loved one will never pay attention to you ever again. How long will this relationship last? Not long.

Without the constant exchange of thoughts, communication of feelings, and demonstration of trust that comes from listening to one another, even the strongest relationship cannot survive. Now picture the most important organizations in your life! It might be your church, your family, and your company. I think that every human organization is like a constellation of individual human relationships. A family is constituted of the relationship of a mother and father, and each of their relationships to the children. A company is the sum of the relationships of executives to team, manager to employee, peer to peer, workers to clients, and sales professionals to prospects. The vitality of these individual relationships compounds to become the overall health and prognosis for the larger organization.

Without the constant exchange of thoughts, communication of feelings, and demonstration of trust that comes from listening to one another, even the strongest relationship cannot survive.

I began to provide training in negotiation principles to private sector firms many years ago. After a few seminars in different industries, I began to realize a profound truth about the importance of listening. The health of any organization reflects the health of the individual relationships between the employees and managers, customers, partners, and vendors. The fate of each relationship rests on how well one person listens to another. If sales staff don't listen to prospects, service technicians don't listen to customers, peers don't listen to each other, and managers don't listen to their teams everything begins to die slowly for that firm. If the members of a family stop listening, the family will drift apart.

The final grade for a hostage negotiator's listening acumen is typically awarded in hours. The final grade for everyone else plays out on a longer timeframe, but the risk and reward of listening for everyone is ultimately life or death.

The final grade for everyone else plays out on a longer timeframe, but the risk and reward of listening for everyone is ultimately life or death.

This harsh reality is the foundation of my book. Listening skills sustain human relationships and human institutions like your business, non-profit organization, city, church, or family. When listening slowly fades and dies, so do the relationships we desperately crave.

Here's the coolest thing. Imagine what happens if someone latched on to listening as a sacred calling. It could be you. What if you happened upon eight active listening techniques and dedicated your professional life to becoming an authentic, intentional listener? What if you convinced one of your colleagues to do the same? What if two people in a family or workplace set out to master this skill we call listening? I propose to you that everything would change for the better. What if each of you found someone else to join in this listening journey? Now you are four. Everyone finds a partner again and now there are eight aspiring master listeners.

In short order, you all would be transforming workplaces into storytelling halls. Everyone would get the strong sense that they were welcome to talk about tough topics, provide feedback to leadership, and explore unspoken opportunities. All of this happens through a simple commitment that begins with you. That's the power of listening, and that's the power of a listening culture.

3. MORE CAMPFIRES

the proper listening environment

"The mass of men lead lives of quiet desperation."
—*Henry David Thoreau*

S ince the stakes are life or death, listening well is one of the most powerful things we can do for another person! I propose to you that everyone you know has a story to tell. You, me, your team at work, your loving family, the homeless guy with a sign hanging out on the street corner, and the woman in front of you at the grocery store check-out stand all have a complex and compelling story of self. Never take these people for granted.

In my listening journey, I have discovered something. There seem to be three types of storytellers. The first group of people have no problem finding an audience. They freely share their story even at times that are inappropriate. They have few filters or boundaries in disclosing what you or I might find intensely private. These people are rare.

Most people fall into the second group. They are willing to share and merely need an invitation and the right circumstances. They have a rich tale that will prove insightful for their leaders if only those leaders will ask. When the time is right, and the audience is clamoring, the fire will be lit, and the story will come.

Unfortunately, I find that a significant number of these stories are left untold. We miss the opportunity to invite their telling.

The third group is afraid. They have been jaded by poor listening and bad relationships from the past. They guard their stories like the treasures they are. All these potential story-tellers are in search of a listener worthy of the sort of trust needed to handle such a precious narrative.

Authentic, intentional listening is so valuable because it is so rare. Some people go through their whole lives and never tell their story. As a hostage negotiator, I get a peek into this world of silent storytellers. My job as a crisis negotiator might be as simple as inviting people to tell stories that they've hidden from the world for decades.

In one instance, my team and I successfully negotiated the release of a hostage and then the surrender of the hostage taker. The suspect had a long history of violence and anti-government sentiment. He told me, "I'll never trust you" at the beginning of the standoff. I invited him to tell his story. I asked insightful questions. I reflected on his answers and gave him respect when he was not inclined to expect it. The ending came as it began to rain. He let the hostage go free. Then he surrendered and was handcuffed- bound for jail and then prison. I went out in the rain to meet him and thank him for doing the right thing. He wanted a hug! He told me that he thought I was the first person who ever listened to him.

It is a stinging indictment of our society that a 30-something-year-old man could sincerely feel that no one had ever heard his story. I was both happy and sad. Happy that I could help the hostage and this man, but sad that he could have gone this long without telling his story. He is not alone. If you read this book and decide to take the path of a master listener, you'll have no shortage of business.

Sometimes we need an anchoring image in our mind to focus our intention. The best image for the sort of listening that I'm talking about is that of a roaring campfire.

Sometimes we need an anchoring image in our mind to focus our intention. The best image for the sort of listening that I'm talking about is that of a roaring campfire.

Inside the circle of the light, it's safe to tell your story for all to hear. Almost any topic can be discussed in this atmosphere of friendship and trust. Outside the circle, there is darkness, fear, and confusion. Leaders and lovers should put considerable time and energy into creating a campfire atmosphere at work or in the home! Stoke the coals, throw on a new log, and invite the story-telling to commence.

If you aspire to love or lead other people, then you have a duty to learn how to listen. Listening is not a fad. Listening is the oldest skill in addition to the ultimate skill. It is right and just that you should be reading this brief primer on listening well in an age of radical connectivity. Despite all these technological advances, the campfire still reigns supreme.

I'm convinced that there will never be a substitute for a real, live, breathing, heart-pumping human sitting across from you and training their whole being like a radar on you- ready to receive. I hope you want to enshrine listening in your home. I propose that you should be the leader who builds roaring campfires where teams gel, ideas are exchanged and implemented, sales are made, and respect is given. This book is written with that intention in mind.

What should motivate all of us to become the best listener we can is this truth. We should listen to people because of what they are, not who they are. We listen to people because as a human being they possess a dignity that is invaluable. They are one of us! If we want to be excellent, we won't choose to listen to only the people that are like us in appearance or ideology. We won't choose to listen to someone for what we can use them for. We listen to give respect to a fellow human. Life's tough. Make friends. Especially since as members of the same species, we are so alike!

We should listen to people because of what they are, not who they are. We listen to people because as a human being they possess a dignity that is invaluable.

---

4. RADICALLY SIMILAR

why <u>everyone</u> needs listening

"If you could see humanity spread out in time, as God sees it, it would look like one single growing thing—rather like a very complicated tree. Every individual would appear connected with every other."
—C.S. Lewis

My crisis negotiations have put me on the phone and face-to-face with drunks, drug addicts, gunmen, jumpers, teens, adults, veterans, and the mentally ill. They were rich and poor, men and women, and of all races and creeds. Some seemed like monsters. All were broken. All were unique. My corporate training and consulting embrace a different collection of folks in the world- business owners, executives, professionals, and employees of all sorts. The diversity of the people and situations I've encountered is a beautiful gift. With this rich diversity of differences, it is tempting to think that people have little in common.

I believe the opposite is true. Human beings are radically similar. Despite the full range of appearances between the genders and the races and ethnicities, and the complex diversity of human beliefs and cultures, there is a "greatest common denominator" for every member of humanity. What we share makes us radically similar. I use the term "radical similarity" because this one thing that is the same can overshadow all that is different. Every human being wants to be understood and loved. Everyone has a story to tell and desires an audience, even an audience of one. Understanding this similarity is critical for the aspiring student of the listening craft.

> *Every human being wants to be understood and loved. Everyone has a story to tell and desires for an audience, even an audience of one.*

The human need to be heard and valued trumps most everything else. Even when we twist these desires and hurt those who might love and understand us, we demonstrate those needs. That's why I know that the techniques I will share with you in this book will work for you if you will work at them.

This book is a product of my experiences as a hostage negotiator and mental health response officer for a large police department. The field of police crisis negotiations is not old. We can trace its origins back to the Munich Olympic Games of 1972. Members of the Black September terror group took a portion of the Israeli Olympic delegation hostage. The West German authorities ended the crisis using force. Eleven athletes and coaches, all but three terrorists, and a West German police officer were killed.

In the aftermath of Munich and several other high profile barricades in New York, the New York Police Department sent Lieutenant Frank Bolz and a Detective-psychologist Harvey Schlossberg to conduct a post-event critique. Since New York City is a popular target for terrorism, the NYPD had an interest in learning from the tragedy of the Olympic siege. Bolz and Schlossberg came to a few conclusions. They thought little effort was given to negotiating a peaceful surrender or to buying more time for a better tactical plan. They also thought the lack of trained, professional people who could negotiate contributed to the ineffective dialogue. Upon returning to New York, they began forming the first police crisis negotiation unit that would create a new option in resolving the worst sorts of criminal and terrorist sieges.

Before Munich, the options for the police or military when confronted with a hostage crisis were:

- Snipers – shoot the bad guy(s) when they poke their head up;
- Kick in the door and go in shooting the bad guy(s);
- Use explosives and/or chemical munitions to make the bad guy(s) evacuate.

I chuckle when I see contemporary management styles that are still "pre-Munich". There are still leaders who think they can "make" their teams produce consistent, high-quality work. Those days are gone. Any such attempt would have to solve the problem of motivating unmotivated people. Authority and discipline make poor motivators. We will discuss the prime role of listening and influence rather than brute force in management. Look for it in *Chapter 12: Influence.*

After Munich, the fourth and best option became the negotiated release of hostages and the surrender of the hostage takers. Early negotiators learned to use simple strategies to listen deeply to their subjects. They relied heavily on bargaining techniques and active listening to defuse dangerous sieges.

After Munich, the fourth and best option became the negotiated release of hostages and the surrender of the hostage takers.

Negotiation principles are here to stay. Buying time is the basis for negotiating. The radical philosophy pioneered by NYPD's Hostage Negotiation Team quickly began to spread throughout the country and then the world. When I became a negotiator, those same principles were the foundation of my training. They influenced the inner workings of the Federal Bureau of Investigation. The FBI is the gold standard for negotiation training and operational culture in the world of law enforcement and counter terrorism units.

Gary Noesner was the FBI's unit chief for their Crisis Negotiations Unit headquartered in Quantico, Virginia. Gary credits the NYPD efforts led by Schlossberg and Bolz with incorporating bargaining and stalling tactics in their efforts to resolve hostage crises. Noesner was trained by these two NYPD pioneers.

When the evidence became clear in the early 1990s that In an effort to enhance their efforts in kidnapping for ransom and hostage barricade negotiations, the FBI took the NYPD philosophy of stalling for time* and added the teachings from psychologist Carl Rogers, knowledge from the professional counseling community, and the FBI's own lessons in negotiation. This enhancement is essentially the active listening skills that have become the basis for modern crisis negotiations training. This is my own heritage as a negotiator. I have trained hundreds of negotiators to use the active listening principles to save lives all over the world.

Noesner would go on to formulate the FBI Behavioral Change Stairway Model using the active listening skills as the risers supporting each step. This model guides negotiators in making a connection to a suspect or subject in order to gain compliance and a surrender.

Since Munich, these basic principles and the framework surrounding them that emphasize empathy, rapport, and influence have been used to change human behavior. I am convinced that these listening guides work so well because they meet people right where they are.

When used properly, these techniques are the most effective method I've ever seen to calm emotions, build rapport, demonstrate empathy, and influence behavior. The techniques are simple and harness the universal human desire to be understood, listened to, and loved. By the time you finish this book, you will know and trust these same techniques on your journey to become an excellent listener.

✾ ✾ ✾

* *"Stalling for Time" later became the title for Gary Noesner's excellent autobiography.*

5. EXCELLENCE
IN LISTENING

becoming a master listener

"Anything worth doing, is worth doing badly."   —
G.K. Chesterton

W hen you start at the beginning, try to keep the end in mind. Here you are, at the start of a journey into the heart of listening and leadership. This is a fine place to remind you that our goal should be excellence in listening.

Excellence as a word within the English vocabulary has a rough go of it. A lot of corporate mission statements name excellence as their goal. Attend any leadership training or speech and they will throw around the word "excellence" with abandon. Excellence is a word that we use freely but rarely take the time to define.

As you read this book, you should develop a strong sense that I think defining key terms is critical. My definitions are not ripped from Webster. They come from contemplation about the nature of things. My definitions are rooted in my experience as a leader and follower in many diverse industries. They are influenced mightily by my education as a philosopher and the pragmatic nature of policing and crisis negotiations.

Philosophy insists upon proper definitions. We could gain a lot from examining the words we commonly use in business and life to describe success and leadership. Then we can seek to understand what these words mean in a practical sense. Let's take this crucial concept of excellence and hammer out a working definition.

Excellence is an ancient idea. The classic Greek philosophers knew of it. Plato and Aristotle both spoke of *arête*, a complex understanding of excellence. It incorporates elements of moral virtue, knowledge, and fulfilling one's purpose. Over years of experience, I have developed a working definition of excellence that mirrors *arête*. I propose that excellence means, "Joyfully doing the right thing well". Let us unpack this definition phrase by phrase.

"JOYFULLY...

Excellence is rarely accomplished begrudgingly. Joy is a critical aspect of being great. So many widely acclaimed leaders were acclaimed precisely because they found joy in their craft of leading. Joy in a task is infectious. Joyful leaders mean joyful movements. Joy is a great protection against mediocrity, burnout, and malfeasance.

...DOING...

Excellence is an activity! You can read all the books in the world about leaders and leadership and excellence, but no gains in performance will ever occur until you put them into action. Excellence is measured in some productive process. Take leadership as an example: the harder the work, the greater the need for excellent leadership.

> *[E]xcellence... means, "Joyfully doing the right thing well".*

Some of my most galvanizing experiences leading teams have

come through my work in law enforcement. As a police sergeant, and particularly commanding elite units of specialized police professionals, I had to make split-second decisions in rapidly evolving incidents. I developed my ability to make a hasty plan in a crisis and act decisively. Thinking is not leading. Planning is not leading. Thinking and planning are critical for leaders, but they are not the same as leading. Consistently, history's lessons of excellent leadership avoid the opposing extremes of paralysis and rashness. Perfect is the enemy of greatness. Leaders seize the moment, take risks, and do the best thing right now. It is the same in any endeavor where excellence is the goal. Especially listening.

...THE RIGHT THING...

The next element in our definition ties excellence to moral virtue, just like Aristotle would. How can a leader be great if they are morally bankrupt? Again, consider the case of an excellent leader. A leader who is not morally sound is not a leader, they are a dictator. No matter how benevolent the dictatorship, there can be little success when followers are bullied, jaded, and their good is ignored.

Leaders sustain their organizations by possessing moral clarity and being people of integrity. When followers know where their leader stands because of consistent vision and behavior, they can honestly commit to the leader's cause. When a leader continually reads tea leaves to know what is good, followers will withhold their commitment out of confusion. Leaders know that integrity is the basis for trust. Victory at any cost is a terrible rallying cry for those who pay the price. If anyone uses a talent, no matter how impressive it is, for evil, I do not think they are performing excellently.

...WELL."

An aspiring leader of excellence might be joyful, act decisively and with integrity, but what about being effective? Excellence demands moral clarity. It respects the process of continual improvement and embraces tough feedback. Results matter. Excellence allows for instances of losing only if there is some value taken from the loss. Excellence is the process of persistent improvement. Leaders must be relentless in analyzing performance and becoming an expert in the task at hand.

We just unpacked the working definition of excellence. The unpacking reveals insight into each aspect of the concept we call excellence. You are ready to joyfully do the right thing well when it comes to masterful listening!

This is a great time to talk about perfection. First, it doesn't exist. Things can always get better. Also, things can always get worse. There's no such thing as human perfection in this life. Second, obsession with perfection often leads to failure. Focusing on eliminating all mistakes leads to more mistakes. Fear of making a mistake can paralyze someone mastering a new craft. Mistakes are the stuff that substantial improvement is made of! Third, listening is a process that involves other people and their brokenness. It is not perfected. Through a constant process of improvement, it can be mastered. A master listener is not error-free. A master listener is adept at minimizing the damage of a mistake and turning it into an opportunity for empathy, humility, and building rapport.

...obsession with perfection often leads to failure. Focusing on eliminating all mistakes leads to more mistakes. Fear of making a mistake can paralyze someone mastering a new craft.

G.K. Chesterton famously wrote that "Anything worth doing is worth doing badly". He understood that something so important as trying to listen better should not be delayed. Practice doesn't make perfect. Proper practice, that is, intentional and intelligent practice, makes for continual improvement. That's excellence. That's our goal. We can't delay the beginning of this process waiting for the perfect time or pre-conditions.

I work with aspiring leaders and emerging stars in companies who have been told they need to work on their "communication ability". I chuckle. What is that? After many such conversations with articulate, educated people, I convince them that this sort of ambition is too vague to produce results. What I recommend is to become a better communicator by becoming a better listener. Now I can give them a proven framework for the process of becoming a skilled, intentional listener. If people sense a deficiency in your communications, do not take this to mean you should talk more. Usually, the proper diagnosis is listening failure. Focus on this, and excellence in communication is within reach.

Excellence is best pursued with a clear concept in our mind of what the end state should be. Good philosophy starts with great definitions. For the next two chapters, we will focus on clearly defining what listening is and is not. Thus, we begin an examination of listening for leaders and lovers with this end in mind: to become excellent.

6. NOT LISTENING

false listening;

PLUS a brief, 8 question self-test to determine if you are, in fact, already a master listener

"You're short on ears and long on mouth."   —
John Wayne

I raise chickens. Fowl are fierce and simple. Rattle the feed bucket across the yard, and they come running and flapping because they have excellent hearing. Hearing is a physiological process. It begins out in the world as objects in our environment move and create vibrations in the air. These vibrations travel in sound waves to our ears. The structure of the ear elegantly interfaces with our central nervous system. The vibrations are translated into nerve impulses and travel to the brain. We interpret these impulses based upon our experience to know what those moving things are. This process is incredible and beautiful, but hearing is not listening.

The hearing process sounds amazing until you realize that chickens can do it. As I tell my five children- be better than chickens. You even hear in your sleep! How else would your alarm clock wake you? Please don't misunderstand. Hearing is a wonderful gift. It's just not the sort of human activity that heals wounds, seals relationships, and unites factions. It does not lead to excellence in communication.

Hearing is not the same thing as listening. It's unintentional, unmotivated, and haphazard. It's a false listening that gathers words not knowledge. Hearing when done by humans is "auto-pilot listening" that usually misses emotions and main ideas and turns away storytellers.

Mindless hearing manifests itself in many ways in modern life. People might mistakenly think they are listening when they are watching movies, enjoying music, or binge-watching streaming shows online. I call this form of "listening" by a specific name: consuming. As audio and video consumers, we are not participating in the communication process. Listening to me is active and needs communication flowing in more than one direction.

Digital media consumption is how we spend a lot of our time nowadays. I am afraid it is killing our listening skills by training our minds to be antennae for pleasing sights and sounds. Real people rarely match the production value of a professionally edited video. We hesitate to share our fears, dreams, and aspirations with each other. When we do, it is often raw, unfiltered, and incomplete. We need to reclaim the faculties of our intellect that allow us to deeply attend to others when they are communicating under stress.

In the modern hustle of business and life in general, our society lowers the bar for listening. Most leaders don't take the time or use intentional techniques to become exceptional listeners. Listening has become so rare that genuinely attending to another will make you stand out. It will make people feel listened to, understood, and loved. This fulfills the universal desire that is the "radical similarity" of humanity detailed in *Chapter 4: Radically Similar*.

In the modern hustle of business and life in general, our society lowers the bar for listening.

Our shared human desire for connection is what makes the fine art of "listening well" so compelling. It is the secret to unlocking the universe of people. It is foundational for both leadership and friendship. Poor listening is almost universally despised for the same reason. Isn't it true that you generally know good listening from poor listening when you are on the receiving end? And isn't it true that we have a hard time articulating the difference in an entirely rational sense?

Does your spouse or close friend know when you are *really* listening? They do. You also know someone is not listening to you. There are clues to another person's attentiveness we can observe. Perhaps they reveal their lack of listening through poor posture or absence of eye contact. In the end, I think it is mostly intuitive. Somehow, we just know. Leaders would do well to remember that their employees, clients, and loved ones all have this innate ability to sense when leaders are not listening.

With the deck stacked against the aspiring listener, it can be difficult to try. It can seem that no one is listening. So many of our problems in the boardroom and living room can be boiled down to poor listening.

It doesn't have to be that way. If excellent listening is a mansion, I want to be the wise architect to help you build the best home for your listening skills. The problem is that we usually start in a fixer-upper and must do some demo work first. You'll need to swing the proverbial sledgehammer.

Through my workshops, keynotes, and executive coaching sessions, I've learned something important. Every audience or client I work with wants to be a good listener. Most think they are good enough already. Nearly all are afraid to know the truth. To build your listening skillset right, we need to pull some sheetrock off your walls, peel up the carpet, and see all the ugly. Everyone I've worked with has had a few bad listening habits. So here are the eight most common poor listening habits. I highly recommend you give yourself an honest appraisal. Answer these questions:

Everyone I've worked with has had a few bad listening habits.

---

1. Do you listen to hear what is being said, or do you listen to understand what is being meant?

Listening well means listening for the emotions, meanings, and messages that the other person is expressing. Often the other person cannot articulate these thoughts in plain language. They may even test you to see if you care enough to notice. In any event, listening without understanding is poor listening. We can do better.

In the next chapter we will explore eight active listening skills. The magical effect of these reliable techniques is to help drill down into the precious treasures of what others tell us. Emotions, values, motivations, fears, and influences are just some of these valuable hidden messages.

There is incredible trust gained when we listen well, hear the true message, and reveal this fact to our speaker. Your credibility as a listener is damaged when you find yourself saying, "I'm listening!" Good listeners don't say that. They reveal the unspoken messages to show how well they listened. If you don't do this out of habit, then now is the time to start! I will give you some strategies to improve in *Chapter 19: Insightful Listening.*

2. Do you interrupt?

Interrupting sends a clear message to our communication partner. "What you have to say is not as important as what I have to say!" Want to fail at listening? Just start interrupting. Interrupting is consistently the most despised of the poor listening habits in this list. It causes a strong emotional reaction in the interrupted. Assertive folks will take you to task. The more reserved will simply stop telling you anything to avoid being interrupted. Remember the image of the campfire! We are called as leaders and lovers to stoke the flames. By interrupting, you just poured a big bucket of water on the fire!

Interrupting is consistently the most despised of the poor listening habits in this list. It evokes strong emotional reaction.

Interruptions happen so often in our lives that we all have experience interrupting and being interrupted. Remember the last time someone interrupted you at a time when you were sharing your story? Recall your emotion upon being interrupted. Now consider the effect of that event over time.

The real problem with interrupting others is the deeper message we send. When I interrupt, I signify that "I'm more important than you". Sending this message kills listening, blocks consensus, and breaks trust. You won't have room for interrupting in your listening life. Ditch it.

3. Do you "one-up" others' stories?

Imagine I told you a story about my recent fishing trip to a local reservoir. I caught a 15-pound channel cat! Can you believe that? "Sure," you say, "it would be a little smaller than the 20- pound Muskie I caught on my recent trip to the boundary waters in Canada..." That's the classic "one-up". We do it with our successes, failures, and the precociousness of our children. One-upping tells the other, "Nice campfire, but check out this huge bonfire I built!"

"One-upping tells the other, "Nice campfire, but check out this huge bonfire I built!"

Leaders should be careful to avoid the label of a "one-upper". We all have that friend or colleague who always has a story to match ours. These folks have consistently done something or know someone that has done something better than you. A one-upper rarely has the experience of connecting deeply with others during his conversations, since this habit is the opposite of empathy. The topic is continually turning back towards him.

The twisted aspect of the "one-up" is that we think we listened well. We recognized that the topic was fishing and tried to show how much we appreciate the sport. Despite our good intentions, this is poor listening. We took the lazy way out. The great listener would say, "It sounds like you love fishing! Tell me more."

In my workshops, I often get asked if it important for listeners to also share their story with others. If we all want to be heard, loved, and understood, doesn't a habit of active listening stifle this need for us, the intentional listeners? The beauty of being attuned to others in how we communicate with them is the true relationships you build with everyone. In this process, they will be dying to know more about you. They will ask you to share your fish story. Then, and only then, is it a good idea to share your own perspective. It will be genuinely received and add to the trust. This is not a "one-up". This is a sign that your listening is influential.

4. Do you find yourself daydreaming or distracted?

We live in a high-pressure leadership environment. Most of the people in our organization are wearing multiple hats. We are constantly thinking about the next thing on our schedule. Multitasking does not help us become good listeners! How often do we miss critical information as we daydream about our busy schedules? How often do we allow our mind to wander, either to the past or to the busy future? Listening well means focusing on the valuable person and their message being transmitted in the present. The listening leader stays in the now and attends to their communication partners.

We are constantly thinking about the next

thing, as leaders and followers. Multi-tasking does not help us be good listeners!

Daydreaming is bad on its own, but it often contributes to interrupting and "one-upping". Keeping our focus on the other person's story helps us avoid the urge to interject or trump their story with a better version of our own. Human beings are designed and built to continually monitor our environment for new stimuli. Our eyes have a wide range of vision. Our finely-tuned hearing and huge brain can constantly monitor the noisemakers in our world. We have a natural attraction to distraction!

If our listening brain is competing with a distracting environment, listening suffers. The most distracting element of our modern listening arena is digital media. The most distracting of digital media is our smart phone. When you answer your phone in the middle of a conversation with a living breathing human person in front of you, you send them a clear message- "This phone call is more important than you." If you want to be an excellent leader and listener, tame your phone! Turn off the ringer, turn off the TV when listening to people, turn off your computer monitor and speakers. Be the master of your environment and watch people notice.

For leaders, daydreaming can occur when we hear a truth or a new concept that we immediately want to implement in the organization. Don't do that! Wait until the other person shares their ideas completely. Then ask good questions to see what they think about implementation. You'll find they have a lot more to offer than that first intriguing distraction.

5. Do you ask questions like an interrogator?

Proper question selection is the foundation of discovery. Leaders must constantly educate themselves about internal culture conditions and external business climate for productivity and innovation. When questioning your subordinates, do you seek data in bits and bytes? Interrogation is the term I use for asking rapid-fire questions that get short, low-value response. The message we send is like the classic line during an interrogation in an old cop show- "I'll ask the questions here, bud." By tightly controlling the questions, we limit the answers and dominate the flow of information.

> *Proper question selection is the*
> *foundation of discovery.*

Listening well means asking questions that allow others to express themselves fully! Entire concepts, ideas, and emotions will unfold before your very eyes. This makes listening simple. There are many benefits to asking great questions instead of interrogating. We'll explore this in detail in *Chapter 14: Ask Better Questions*. There you will learn all about the active listening technique we call "Open-Ended Questions".

6. Do you listen only long enough to decide what you will say?

We can easily anticipate what others are trying to tell us. It might be a complaint or gripe, or an idea that has been presented to you as a leader what seems like a hundred times before. When we think we know what is being said, we often begin to think of our response before the other person is finished. This is how we miss a new and novel aspect of the communication. Even worse, we might show our partner that we stopped listening halfway through their thought.

Remember that people who share their stories know when we stop listening! Listening entails receiving valuable ideas. Don't buy others' cherished thoughts and feelings at 50% off. If you haven't heard the punctuation mark on the other person's story, it's not your turn yet. I'll discuss an antidote to this bad habit in *Chapter 17: Sometimes Say Nothing*.

7. Do you have to ask others to repeat themselves?

When we don't listen and miss out on critical information, we've failed in listening. It happens. Now, we have a tough choice.

The easy way out is to pretend we listened well and leave the conversation that much poorer. The hard thing to do is to admit we missed out and ask the speaker to repeat themselves. On the one hand, we show we have the proper humility and care enough to get the message. On the other hand, we send a clear message that we weren't listening. Being an excellent listener requires working hard so we are never forced to make that difficult choice. Get it right the first time!

8. Do you give an appropriate response?

When I am working with companies to build their listening culture, invariably some team members oversimplify their efforts to listen better. Their mistake is equating "listening more" with "listening well". Good listeners balance listening and speaking. Imagine the effect of a stony-faced silence greeting your communication partners! A great listener creates a conversation that lets their friends, partners, subordinates, even their foes, have their say. They do this with their attentive silence and with their carefully chosen word.

There are other habits we build as listeners that hold us back from being the best leaders and lovers. I think these are the eight most prevalent and pervasive. We are about to embark on a journey of discovery for great listening skills. Don't bring any extra baggage! Do not let this opportunity pass with mere lip service. Saying, "I wish I were a better listener" will not make it so. Here's your first call to action: recognize the bad listening habit you exhibit most often and focus on reducing this aspect of your listening ability.

Here's your first call to action: recognize the poor listening skill you exhibit most often and focus on this area of your listening ability.

Just pick one! If you try to change too much too fast, you will likely become discouraged and give up. If you feel brave, go ask your boss, your peers, and your direct reports if you listen well. Then ask how your bad listening habits might be slowing your team. Now comes the important task. If you trusted them enough to ask, and they trusted you enough to tell you the painful truth then enlist their help.

Give them permission to correct your poor listening habits. Name the habit you are trying to break. Show them this book and highlight the listening error you want to correct. This is the fastest way I've found to improve listening ability- the gentle correction of someone you respect!

Every time you slip and do that one bad thing you don't want to do anymore, do this- *name it*. Apologize and name what you did. "I am so sorry I just interrupted you. Please continue!" Invite your team to correct you when they see it. Think critically about why you slipped. Make changes in your environment if necessary. One example would be if you get distracted by incoming emails on your PC when listening to others in your office. Simply lock the screen and mute the speakers when in a conversation.

The vast majority of your listening problems are unforced errors in self-mastery. We have a preference for our own perspective, experiences, and narrative. When we hear others share a story, we are naturally disposed to think of our own. Resist this urge. It is natural, but not good. Unless we become motivated and curious as story gatherers, we will never become intentional, excellent listeners.

Now, we're oriented away from merely hearing or consuming others' powerful stories. We are primed to stoke those campfires and scare off our biggest, baddest listening killer. It's time to find out what listening really is.

7. THIS IS LISTENING

a skill, a craft, a habit, a way of life;

PLUS the two, and only two components of listening well

"Talk to me."
—*NYPD Hostage Negotiation Team unit motto*

L ong after my journey to master the art of listening began, I had the good fortune to have my hair cut by a woman who asked what I did for a living. I told her that I am a corporate trainer and keynote speaker. She asked what I taught. I told her, "How to listen well." She stopped snipping and cocked her head to one side. She stared at me skeptically. "So, you *tell* other people how to listen?" I said, "That's about the size of it!" She laughed and asked, "Don't you just have to tell them to shut up and let the other guy talk?"

Nothing could be farther from the truth about the best sort of listening. This book is about major league, capital-L Listening. I call it intentional listening or authentic listening. The practices I discuss in Chapters 14 through 21 are commonly referred to as "active listening skills (ALS)". All these terms attempt to describe the magical experience of someone authentically attending to your words.

Merely hearing is for the birds- literally. Remember to be better than a chicken when listening! Passively consuming the deepest, most intimate beliefs, emotions, and aspirations of our friends and colleagues is a leadership failure. Poor listening is a sign of a person willing to take her chances on whether she succeeds in her career and every essential human relationship. Neither chickens nor the mediocre have any need for the rest of this book. From here on out, you are taking a plunge into listening as a skill, a habitude, and a way of life.

Authentic listening is distinguished from hearing sounds or consuming media by the intention of the listener. Active listeners seek knowledge not data. Authentic listeners are adept at identifying and exploring the emotions and motivation of the speaker. Real listening consists of finding the main idea, not just the supporting words. The measure of the value of this process is the quality and depth of the trust and influence the listener can build with her communications partner. I have found no better way to convert friends from enemies than to listen to them well by speaking less and saying more.

There's something magical about excellent listening. If you can't hear, a scientist can tell you why. If you don't listen, it's not so simple to diagnose. Recall the phenomenon of your significant other and the uncanny ability to know whether you are listening or just hearing. She or he "just knows". They are evaluating you, the listener, for a higher order of attention!

This form of listening is something that is uniquely human. While listening often relies upon our sense of hearing, it is something far more valuable. It is not solely physiological. It is spiritual. Listening is a function of the mind and soul, not the ears. Listening is the foundation of excellence in human communications.

Listening is a function of the mind and soul,

not the ears. Listening is the foundation of excellence in human communications.

Listening is the most crucial skill we use to master the art of living and doing hard work with other people. I am often saddened because listening could be the key to unlocking our potential as leaders and lovers, but you wouldn't know it by the general public's commitment to mastering this skill. For all the importance of listening, there's a dirty little secret about modern Western culture's treatment of such a critical activity. You can see this weak point in how we instruct our children.

There are four basic communication skills: writing, reading, speaking, and listening. Writing is the skill that kids hone last. Our written words tell others a lot about us. Writing well is a fantastic gift. As elementary students, we spent a lion's share of time practicing this craft. As adults, we devote a lot of our day to writing, but not most of our time.

Reading is important too! Reading and writing taken together is literacy, and literacy is the hallmark of civilization. We begin even before formal schooling to learn our alphabet. Every year of your educational life you devoted a considerable amount of time to learning how to read well. Each day of this modern era, you read. Over time, all that reading we are doing gets us somewhere. Reading is important.

Speaking is effortless for you now. Remember back before your school years to recall how and when you learned to speak. You speak often these days in person and on the phone to people regarding subjects of great importance. You probably took a class in high school and college called speech or interpersonal communications. Some of us even join Toastmasters or receive coaching in the art of speechmaking. Schools build assigned speeches or presentations into their curricula because speaking well is a skill that predicts success.

This brings us to listening. It is the first that you learn. You listened in the womb. The explosion of intelligence and self-awareness in your early childhood was fueled by listening. Our early inquiry was fueled by asking lots of "Why" questions and listening intently to the explanations. Regarding cognitive development, we listened long before we could speak, read, or write. Listening comes first in building the internal human communications suite and then it is used throughout the rest of our lives to acquire and hone all other talents, knowledge, and abilities.

Let me repeat that for emphasis! Every skill you have was built on the foundation of listening. I have come to realize that our waking day is essentially a long string of listening opportunities. We should listen far more than we speak, read, or write each day if we want to seize those opportunities.

Here is the dangerous part. Despite all these wonderful opportunities to listen to the amazing people around us, we don't. For all the time and energy poured into speaking, reading, and writing, almost no one studies and practices listening. I make it a point to poll the audiences in my listening training to see who has received formal listening education. The number is never more than 5%. Imagine if less than 5% of the professionals in my audiences had been formally trained to read or write!

For all the time and energy poured into speaking, reading, and writing, almost no one studies and practices listening.

Now we come to the audacious part of my little book on listening. Once you understand their context, my claims that listening is "life or death" and "one of the most powerful things we can do for another person" are easy to digest. Selling the importance of listening in a culture of noise and self-interest is an easy sell. What is tougher is making the case that I can somehow tell you how to become an excellent listener. This is only possible if intentional listening is a skill. My haircutting friend was a skeptic. She is not the only one.

A common objection I face is that there is no way to improve as a listener. I think this is because we all know people who are naturally good listeners and others who are naturally bad listeners. The premise for these objections is that listening is not a skill. Many people believe that listening is an innate talent that resists our efforts for improvement. Some of those skeptics use this belief to resist facing the hard task of improvement. Fortunately for those of us who recognize our poverty in listening ability, I firmly and confidently believe that listening is a skill.

We can all listen to some degree of natural ability. We can all get better. This skill is perishable. Use it or lose it! Anyone can jump into a crisis and negotiate, but excellent negotiators understand that it is a craft that demands rehearsal. Listening well is foundational to everything we do in business and represents the glue for our relationships with our loved ones. It deserves our careful consideration.

I am firmly convinced that listening is a skill and not a natural gift. I have made a living taking beat cops and transforming them into successful hostage negotiators through skills-based training. I have seen similar success in the corporate world as people use these same principles to improve their abilities. When I can show you eight repeatable, reliable ways to get better at listening, it is a compelling case to prove that listening is a skill. Lose your intention, grow complacent, ignore this training, and you will begin to lose your edge. This is true of listening and any other worthy skillset.

Listening is a skill that should become a craft. Many people today do not have the experience of learning a craft. Only a few generations before you and me, everyone learned a craft. Craft means culture. It is a skill that produces value for other people. You will need to work at it. It cannot be learned in a book, even a book as great as the one you are reading right now! It takes trial, error, feedback, and dogged determination.

Craft also means a vocation. Do you think that you can make a living, or improve your financial standing by simply listening well? I dare say yes. No matter what you do, add listening intentionally to what you do and see how the quality of your work product improves. Listening adds value to everything and every process.

You'll need a master to be an apprentice. What guidance I can provide in this book might be enough to start! Seek out other masterful listeners and build up a professional relationship so you have sources of wisdom and craftsmanship. In the heyday of craftmanship, crafts like blacksmithing were handed down generationally. A blacksmith descended from a long line of blacksmiths! Like blacksmithing, I think masterful listening is a skill that can be handed from one person to another.

My first mentor in the negotiating industry is fond of asking new trainees, "How good do you want to be?" He meant that you must commit to this hard and noble work. As a skill and craft, listening is simple but hard. If you want to know the secret to the universe of people, I can tell you in two words: Listen better. Work hard! It is a simple proposition. Too bad it's not easy!

Listening well is not a complex task. Unfortunately for you and me, we find ourselves in an anti-listening age. We live in a world of cacophony! With all this idle talk and digital distraction, it appears that the art of listening is dying. Right now, let us begin to treat listening as the ultimate skill for helping people. To understand this skill better, we can dive deeper into the stuff that listening is made of.

We live in a world of cacophony! With all this idle talk, digital media, and social noise, it appears that the art of listening is dying.

In keeping with my "listening is simple" theme, there are only two components to listening well. Excellence in listening requires the listener to:

1. be attentive, *and*

 2. provide an appropriate response.

That's it! Just two steps, repeated over and over until the story is complete and the campfire dies a natural, satisfying death! Unfortunately, this is also in keeping with my "listening is hard" theme. Keeping our focused attention on someone's story requires discipline and motivation. Providing an appropriate response takes some training and practice. Both tasks can become second nature as you build up your listening skillset.

Attentiveness is the first component of listening well. Your head has two ears, two eyes, a nose, and a mouth. Inside your head is the brain, and somehow (and no one knows precisely how yet) you have an intellect and a will nestled metaphysically in that brain and its assisting organs. I can't explain how all that works, but let's just go with it for now, because you are going to need all those sensory and nervous system organs and your "mind" with its intellect and will to be attentive.

Attentiveness is an intentional act of your will. You must decide to pay attention, and then you must hold yourself to the commitment until the time for listening is done. This internal commitment should change your external appearance! Your head should pivot to focus on the source of the listening stimulus, your valuable partner in storytelling. Your ears are now oriented to maximize hearing which should aid listening. Your eyes should make eye contact. Soften your face, now. Smile! Good! Check your posture. Uncross your arms, relax, orient your body to match your head. You are now in the proper position to receive an amazing story.

This internal decision causes external changes in your appearance. These cues you send to the external world can now have the added benefit of changing the mind and appearance of other people including potential storytellers. Attentiveness is a real component of listening. Being attentive helps you hear words better. Attentiveness also demonstrates your desire to listen to the other person, increasing their motivation to tell the whole story!

Without creating the perception that you sincerely value

their information, communication stops. Attentiveness is under-valued in a society of multitaskers, but there is no substitute. Consider this: when was the last time you had a meal with other adults without someone checking their Smartphone? I will give you a practical technique to boost your attentiveness in *Chapter 15: Rewarding Storytellers.*

Listening has an equally important second component. Once you attentively receive the message, you should respond in a way that moves the storytelling ahead. Great listening is not just being quiet. If you remain quiet at the wrong moment the entire deli-cate dance of storytelling and inquiry falls apart.

Attentiveness is undervalued in a society of multi-taskers, but there is no substitute. Consider this: when was the last time you had a meal with other adults without someone checking their Smartphone?

Imagine you bare your soul to someone about one of your pas-sions. Your listener is attentive while maintaining eye contact, an open posture, and a pleasant appearance. You pause in your story-telling, and the other person just stares at you pleasantly. You keep going for a little bit more, and again they stare at you without a comment. Sound creepy? It is, and that will kill sharing.

As creepy as a blank stare seems, there are worse ways to react. We are all guilty at times of an inappropriate response: changing the subject, telling our own story, misunderstanding, or even missing the main point. Another inappropriate response is to invalidate another person's experience, emotion, or perspec-tive. You don't have to agree with everyone all the time, but we can receive their thoughts with warm, positive regard. This keeps the avenue of communication open and flowing.

> *You don't have to agree with everyone*
> *all the time, but we can receive their*
> *thoughts with warm, positive regard.*

In fact, active listening as practiced by hostage negotiators is the ultimate method of gracefully disagreeing with another person. We show respect and demonstrate that we properly understand their valued beliefs even when we do not subscribe to those beliefs. When it is our turn, we clearly communicate our perspective. If these two positions are incompatible, we can explore negotiated compromise. At all times we preserve the relationship, model calmness, and give people time to be rational about the situation.

Listening well requires us to provide responses that match the message we receive. This might be any of eight active listening techniques you will soon read. They have been tested over time to provide the best possible response and to encourage more sharing. Maturing as a great listener means practicing until we instinctively choose the best response to keep the story going. This is the equivalent of throwing another log on the campfire.

If we make attentiveness and appropriate response the natural way we engage others, then we no longer have just a skill. We have a habit. We have changed our rudimentary skill into a reflexive skill. Over time, this skill of active listening is sharpened and refined to become the natural way we communicate with people. In the process, we can gain something even more valuable as a student of the listening craft- a reputation.

Think about your own company or any sort of organization you have joined. In your organization, you can spot bad listeners and good listeners. Based on this listening skill status, members will decide whether to confide in this person or not. Storytellers are always sizing up the audience. The members of your organization you consider good listeners tend to be better informed, knowledgeable, and respected.

Listening is a skill, a craft, a habit, and ultimately a way of life. If you always embrace these techniques to be an intentional listener, you will master your craft and people will sit up and take notice. Good things will follow. People love leaders who listen! Being a sounding board for a significant number of people in an organization gives the master listener a game-changing level of influence on the corporate culture. Use it wisely.

8. LEADERS WHO LISTEN

a love story

"The greater the feeling of responsibility for the person, the more true love there is." —
Karol Wojtyla

This book represents the culmination of my years of experience as a hostage negotiator, commander of a small team of elite investigators, and corporate consultant in national circulation. Since 2008, I have been translating my experiences and lessons to the private sector. I've been blessed to work with leaders and their teams in a wide variety of companies and industries all over the country. As I have traveled, I have learned that the art of listening well is crucial for two groups of people: leaders and lovers.

First, this book is for leaders. There are leaders all around me. When it comes to leadership, I cast a wide net. If you lead a Fortune 500 company as a powerful CEO, command a military unit in harm's way, captain your sports team, pastor a church, or raise a family, you're a leader. I subscribe to the somewhat unorthodox belief that all it takes to be a leader is accepting the title. If you claim to be a leader and begin to lead, then you are a leader after all! I don't think leadership is tied to authority.

Unfortunately, there's no certifying body for leadership quality. I've been the victim of poor leadership and suspect you have been too. I've also been inspired and challenged to develop myself as a better worker and person by exceptional leaders. I suspect you have been too! These mentors and sages often had no formal authority over me at the time.

Authority and leadership are not the same. All my bosses have exercised authority over me. Some had the qualities of a great leader. I have also had amazing peers and subordinates who were exceptional leaders. They had no authority over my work, but they inspired me to be better. Authority is something the organization grants. Leadership is an intentional activity that each of us can embrace or avoid.

Having authority does not make you a leader. Being a leader does not mean you have authority, but there is a relationship between the two. Authority creates a duty. It raises the stakes for leadership. It obliges those with authority to listen authentically. To put it another way, everyone *can* lead. Those with authority *should* lead. Sadly, many do not. I think this is because many do not know what leadership is, nor what it is made of.

Leadership is a complex, risky activity. I think there are many skills that great leaders possess. Problem solving, negotiating, and strategizing are critical. Listening with intention is the most important of star in this constellation of skills that make excellent leadership. This book seeks to provide the knowledge and motivation for exceptional leadership through listening.

Second, this book is for lovers. I do not mean sappy sitcom or TV romance love. I am not referring to the love espoused by my 10-year-old son Ray when he says, "I love pizza!" I mean authentic and sacrificial love. This kind of love can build a marriage, a family, or a company. This sort of love can weather any storm. Love in this sense means that you, the lover, "decide and act to increase the good" of your beloved. You sacrifice. You bear hardship. You ease pain for your beloved. That is the sort of love we all need. It's a fundamental requirement of leadership. If you don't love your people and will that they become better tomorrow than they are today, what sort of leader are you?

If you don't love your people and will that they become better tomorrow than they are today, what sort of leader are you?

Listening is a loving act. It might be the most powerful act of service you can perform for another person. This book is about mastering listening to love one another better. This book is for leading and loving people well. I'll wager you want to be excellent at both. If I'm right, then read on.

Listening, loving, and leading all have something in common. There's a lot of folks who are supposed to be doing these things and there are a lot of folks just making a minimal, unintentional effort. The bar is set low with authentic listening, loving, and leading. Doing something is not necessarily doing it well. Having a random positive outcome in a single case is not the same as performing that crucial task with excellence daily.

My training and experiences as a police officer and corporate consultant make me passionate about effective leadership. I know the leader's role in safety and productivity in any sort of human endeavor. As I made my journey of discovery of what good listening requires, I began to understand my leadership strengths and weaknesses. That's why I started speaking publicly about core skills that I felt the best leaders possessed: listening, negotiating, managing performance, and cultivating healthy corporate cultures.

Some leaders are excellent; many are not. The value of this book lies in diagnosing the difference. In other words, what do great leaders have that not so great leaders do not? Are there barriers to leadership excellence? Are there enemies standing in our way as we seek to improve our ability to lead well?

I've worked with hundreds of audiences of all sorts. One of the most enlightening moments in my workshops is when I grab a marker and paper and the students call out the attributes they desire in a leader. There are always a few constants. These perennial favorites all have a direct relationship with skillful listening. Here is a short list of those qualities everyone wants in a leader and the relationship of those attributes to the listening craft.

Humble

We desire leaders who are humble. People want to know that their leader will listen to their good ideas and heed their warning of future ills. If a leader is not approachable, followers will cut off the flow of critical information back to the top. Kill the messenger too many times, and all the messengers stop coming to see you! That is the most dangerous scenario facing a leader who doesn't listen. I call this "insulated leader syndrome". Without honest feedback from the most important people in the organization, the executive functions of decision-making and forecasting will fail. Humility is the quality of a leader that helps them receive feedback without emotion.

If a leader is not approachable, followers will cut off the flow of critical information back to the top. Kill the messenger too many times, and all the messengers stop coming to see you!

In my experience, when an employee offers a tough message and is punished for it through rejection or worse, being blamed for the problem unjustly, they stop providing the bad news. They will let the leader find out naturally. A leader who is not humble is often the sort of leader who runs from emergency to emergency in their corporate culture. This is because routine malfunctions or miscues turn into raging crises when followers are afraid to report bad news. If they feel like their suggestions for improvement are ignored, ridiculed, or worse- stolen, they will ignore this critical obligation to keep their leader informed. Once a significant number of their followers stop providing these critical communications, the leader is trapped in a cocoon of their design. Therefore, listening well is the first and most important task of an authentically approachable leader.

Being approachable implies a certain level of being vulnerable. These are hallmarks of a humble leader. Leaders who try to maintain an image of perfection don't usually make themselves approachable. Not all leaders can say "I didn't know that, thank you," or "I appreciate that criticism. I know it is not easy to tell me that. Thank you." If yours can't, I'd wager you don't find them very approachable. That's a shame. Leaders with humility get better at leading through this gentle correction of their team. The only response to the honest criticism of your subordinate is "Thank You."

Consistent

We desire leaders who are consistent. Teams can innovate and improve so long as they have a sense of security about their future. For many, this foundation is a leader who serves with integrity. It is a huge relief when I know the values and preferences of my leader. I can look at a new problem and have confidence in what the leader would expect me to do. If, as a leader, I present a consistent set of expectations and ethics, my team doesn't need to rely on my spoken word in every situation. This leads to more delegated work and efficiency.

How does listening come into play with consistency? Leaders must make an intentional effort to listen to their team to see if expectations have been communicated properly, and the members trust the leader's consistency. Listening should also be used to determine if there is an environment of innovation and self-reliance.

The political will of the workspace leader is often interpreted by the team as consistency. If the leader bends like a reed to change values or expectations based on the whims of clients or a higher authority in the organization, consistency dies. If the leader changes moods like an emotional chameleon, there can be no innovation. Fickle leadership breeds minimalism. Employees will follow the last order, and only that order will be done. When the leader is inconsistent, no one looks for a better process or more work because every additional task or interaction risks the wrath of the inconsistent leader.

Fickle leadership breeds minimalism.

Lastly, consistency means words and actions complement each other. The most powerfully influential leaders I have followed have let their "yes" mean "yes" and their "no" mean "no". They reserved their commentary for the critical moments and chose their words with care. If they said they would do something or not do something, they developed a reliable system to ensure they followed through. They asked for everyone's input and then they spoke last.

Inspirational

We desire leaders who inspire us. Leaders bring out the best in others. Leadership as an activity is often mistaken for motivating. An attempt to motivate others becomes a trap. Externally motivating an employee would require some compelling force big enough to move them in the short term, but not so terrible that it scars the trust relationship in the long run.

Externally motivating an employee would require some compelling force big enough to move them in the short term, but not so terrible that it scars the trust relationship in the long term.

Fear is one of the most powerful motivating forces for human beings. Fear can cause people to run fast, hide deep, or freeze in their tracks. Leaders should never try to motivate with fear.

Leaders must fight their fears. Leaders also must relieve the fears of everyone around them. The only way I've found to reliably discover and relieve fears is to listen to others well, ask great questions, and show we understand the fear.

The only motivating force I've witnessed that is greater than fear is love. Authentic, sacrificial love trumps fear. I've seen men and women suffer hardships and disregard their fear out of love for their family or friends. Some special people do it for perfect strangers out of love of duty. Listening is a skill and a habit that buttresses love and conquers fear. Through inquiry and empathetic listening, we can know more about our colleagues.

Authentic, sacrificial love trumps fear.

Teams want leaders who create an environment where they are inspired to work hard. They want leaders who get informed about the workspace and what motivates the team. Fear is usually a function of ignorance. The type of love that strikes down fear is founded on sure knowledge of self and the needs of others. Thus, teams want leaders who inspire, not scare, them.

Joyful

We desire leaders who are joyful. As the list grows, my workshop participants often begin to dig deeper for attributes and often use terms like "good sense of humor", "laid-back", "confident", "passionate", and "enjoys leading". These can all be clustered together. I recognize these aspects of a great leader to be under the general heading of joyful.

A joyful leader is protected from a lot of bad habits that grow out of a sense of "burn out" or jadedness. Joy in the work is a pleasure to experience. A healthy dose of joy is infectious. I put it this way- do you want to work for a happy boss in a happy workplace or not?

Work does not have to be dull or dreary. Menial tasks can be done with pleasure when joy is in the work. This sort of joy in the face of the mundane almost always flows down from the leader!

Once I write all these attributes on the board, and a picture of this ideal leader has emerged, the naming of traits grows into a conversation. These conversations tend to center on one thing. This one thing seems to be what team members believe leaders should own. That thing is culture.

9. THE CULTURE BEAST

culture eats everything;

PLUS how to stay off the menu

"For Man was a culture-bearer as well as a soul-bearer, but his cultures were not immortal and they could die with a race or an age . . ." —Walter Miller Jr., A Canticle for Leibowitz

Remember when you learned to ride a bicycle? Think about that process. Chances are, you saw a kid riding a bike somewhere, and this sparked your desire to conquer the skill we call bicycling. Then, someone in your family, like your mom or dad or an older sibling, put you on a bike and gave it a push! If no one at home would help, someone who lived on your block stepped in to be your guide. Very few of us took a 40-hour certification course to learn to ride a bike. This is not just a model for bike-riding! Our most potent, life-long lessons come to us outside of formal education.

That's culture. Informal learning and socialization drive our society. Culture is so powerful and omnipresent in human organizations and society that leaders who ignore it risk their demise! I imagine culture as a ferocious beast. This beast is a living, breath-

DAN OBLINGER

ing creature. It is wild at heart but can be tamed if you're brave. Culture is most like a beast in its appetite. Culture eats everything.

Culture eats your change initiatives and corporate playbook. Unless you have a proverbial finger on the pulse of the culture and build knowledge of culture into your strategies, the untamed culture will feast on any top-down, synthetic course corrections. If you've ever had a great idea for an innovative change in your workspace that failed, and you didn't know why... it was culture. It ate your change initiative.

Culture is bigger than your corporate body! Culture resists formal ownership because so many people outside your company or tribe can influence your culture. Key clients, critical partners, regulatory bodies, and members of the team who have left a legacy can all influence your culture even though they aren't on your payroll. How can we diagnose the ways and depths of this sort of influence? How can we influence the influencers?

Culture eats your formal rules if you let it. Try though we might to create reasonable regulations, there's just too much crucial human activity out there to get it all written into the manual. Culture is what happens when it is not in the book.

Culture is revealed when employees have a problem with no known solution. We tend to look to our left and right at our peers for workarounds, not up to our bosses. A significant number of workers will imitate the behavior of these peers if they think it solves their novel problem. They will do this even if it is clearly not the best long-term solution for the organization. They will break the formal rules to follow the informal cultural norms.

Culture eats your internal educational systems if you allow it. Your organization runs on culture because society runs on this stuff too. The most powerful lessons we gather in our life are usually acquired through cultural learning. Take the bike-riding model and apply it to anything else. How do kids learn to abuse drugs? Someone in the household shows them. If not mom, dad, or sibling, some kid on the block or at school will. Most of the critical things you need to know- the sorts of lessons you've learned and will keep with you for life- will be learned through culture,

52

not formal education.

---

*The most powerful lessons we gather in our life
are usually acquired through cultural learning.*

I know that cultural learning trumps your formal educational systems when your seasoned employees scoff at the "book" learning and say those fateful words- "Let me show you how we *really* do it here." If left alone, your culture will teach a curriculum the executive suite might not endorse!

The existence of a ravenous corporate culture means we ought to be intentional with how we train and educate employees. We should anticipate the intervention of culture and seek to work with it, not against it. Begin the process before you hire and don't stop until your employee separates from the organization completely.

The master listener must respect culture. Recognizing and appreciating the immense force of cultural learning can make listening easier. The most important realization for leaders to make about culture is that it eats everything. Don't fight it! Tame it. Then, you won't be on the menu for the next feeding.

The most important task of the leader in this role of cultural curator is to be intentional in this work. Leaders should think critically about what informs and influences their organizational culture. There are at least four common influences on any culture.

People are at the heart of culture. They are the greatest contributor to your culture. People are the drivers of culture in every discernable culture past and present. This includes the actual members of the group and the memory of those who came before. Some extraordinary humans will continue to influence your culture long after they are gone.

The ethics, desires, fears, values, and goals of each person in your company work together to sculpt the organization's culture. This is a fantastic opportunity for a leader who intentionally listens. Regular listening sessions with key people in your company will offer insights into the health of your corporate culture.

> *The ethics, desires, fears, values, and goals of your culture members drive the lifeblood of the organizational culture.*

If you listen well, to the right people, with the right frequency, you'll hear common themes develop. Whatever a significant number of your people believe is true and do consistently is what forms your culture. Take note and take care that you want these common threads woven into the culture. New people who enter your culture will probably adopt these same beliefs and practices rapidly. If the new hires cannot adapt to the culture, they will not stick around.

While people have the greatest influence, significant historical events can shape the people who in turn craft the culture. Disasters and smashing successes tend to factor heavily in the mix. These seminal events cause trauma or elation. These experiences forge "hard edges" in your culture. The NYPD and FDNY have firm cultural features following their experiences on September 11, 2001. The halo of this event extends even to the Finest and Bravest recruits of this year. That's the power of culture.

The broader culture of the community your organization finds itself in also heavily influences your corporate culture. Your hiring does not happen in a vacuum. Your employees live and work in a context of broader culture with its unique laws and social ways of life. Don't ignore trends around you in the economy and social structures. Those are cultural influences and they will find their way into your "little" culture!

The final cultural influence is the one we control as leaders. The intentional cultivation of culture by those with formal authority can have a significant impact on the health of the company. If leaders leave culture to itself, few good things will follow.

Left alone, culture is wild and untamed. To have the desired effect of aligning work, culture taming must be conducted regularly and energetically! Owners attempt to exert this influence over culture with mission and vision statements, core values, and strategic agendas. Branding and image management are elements of culture cultivation.

The intentional cultivation of culture by the bosses does have a significant impact on the health of the company.

This image of culture as a wild beast is not one of despair. You cannot have two people working together without culture. Culture is not bad! Culture is necessary for human beings to know what to do in most situations. Properly cultivated cultures hold teams together and accomplish audacious goals. Wild beasts might eat you, but tamed monstrosities are what sell out the circus! A well-ordered corporate culture is unmatched in attracting talent and clients, driving innovation, and resisting threats from the outside.

In my experience working with a broad swath of companies and industries, a small percentage succeed in taming their culture. The ones who do make it intentional, intelligent, and incorporate everyone in this task. We'll discuss this more in-depth in *Chapter 22: Building a Listening Culture.*

10. EMPATHY

it's not about you

"Humility is not self-contempt, but the truth about our-selves coupled with a reverence for others; it is self-surrender to the highest goal." —
Fulton Sheen

The foundation for good listening consists of possessing a single attribute and assuring others we possess it. That attribute is empathy. Empathy is the secret ingredient to authentic listening and transformational leadership. The power of empathy remains elusive to many aspiring listeners and leaders because it gets confused with other tools for connecting with others.

Empathy is a powerful and complex concept. Like a crown jewel, it presents many facets when examined from differing angles. In its most distilled definition, empathy is the ability to recognize the perspective and feelings of another person. Empathy includes the ability to see the world through someone else's eyes. For this reason, the master listener is on a quest to silence his own narrative. Aspiring leaders tend to be high-energy and self-motivated folks. It can be a challenge to slow down and thoughtfully reflect on how our demands and directives affect others. Take the challenge. It is worth it.

---

*In its most distilled definition, empathy
is the ability to recognize the perspective
and feelings of another person.*

I can already hear your "Type-A" objections! "But Dan, surely you don't mean that leaders should care about the feelings of their subordinates? Leaders lead, and followers follow, and they'll just have to like it! Weren't you a leader of police officers at the scenes of crimes in progress? Didn't you send men and women into harm's way? Did you stop to ask how they felt?"

Indeed, I am a leader of people who do dangerous things and have sent my subordinates into some tight spots. I didn't ask them how they felt, because I already knew! I had been in their position. More importantly, I took time before these types of incidents to listen deeply to them. I knew what motivated them and what their talents were. We talked about tactics and plans before they were needed. Since I already built up my empathetic understanding to create trust, I could cash in when the chips were down. You can too if you take the time to listen beforehand.

---

*Since I already built up my empathetic
understanding, I could cash in
when the chips were down.*

Empathy doesn't mean we avoid difficult conversations. Leaders demonstrate their capacity for empathy best when the situation is worst. The call to be an empathetic leader demands that we honor and employ this "otherness" in a time of great crisis. By doing so, empathetic communications are transmitted through all the leader's words and actions.

Empathy can be confused with sympathy. I'm more convinced than ever that Hallmark got it wrong. They should have an aisle full of empathy cards, not sympathy. Empathy is more effective, safer to employ, and works across all human boundaries of gender, race, age, culture, religion, and ethnic origin. Sympathy, particularly for strangers or acquaintances, often proves to be a trap.

My favorite illustration of the difference in value between empathy and sympathy involves a pain in your thumb! Have you ever hit your thumb with a hammer? If so, you might be positioned to help anyone who experiences this painful process in the future. Let's see how that might play out:

Dan: "YEOW!"

Donny: "Hey buddy, looks like you just hit your thumb with a hammer!"

Dan: "YES!"

Donny: "Well, the pain is excruciating for a few moments, but it will quickly subside to a throbbing. You will feel that for a few hours, and then your thumbnail will fall off."

Dan: "Thanks, I guess? OWWW!"

That will not work! Perhaps providing a guided itinerary of pain is not the best strategy. The attempt by my fictional pal Donny to help his buddy Dan might be better described as sympathy. This Greek word literally means that Donny and Dan are feeling the same. There's a natural, reasonable motivation for Donny to share his experience that matches a similar situation with Dan. Donny has a relevant experience. Many leaders do when their subordinates are facing a challenge! The problem is that Dan just doesn't care. The trap with problem-solving, sympathy, or the relevant historical perspective our leaders can bring to bear on our problems is that the person in need of this help must be rational and ready to accept the aid.

In a crisis, reason and problem-solving are in short supply. Great listeners learn to begin with empathy and listening. It gives the other person time to reduce their negative emotions and become rational. Some of the dynamics that impede problem-solving are best resolved with the active listening skills in Chapters 14 to 21.

Empathetic leaders build the best teams, spur retention and development, and are rarely ambushed by crises because their teams are not afraid to communicate openly about problems before they explode. Empathy should be the default response of a skilled leader and an excellent listener.

One obstacle to true empathy could be a reluctance to accept people for who they are and where they are in their journey through this crazy life. We train police negotiators to have warm, positive, unconditional regard for people. This can be unpleasant when they don't share your values or beliefs. The valuable folks we will engage in listening might just disappoint us with an emotional attack, distasteful opinion, or personal criticism. Listen to them anyway. Look past any internal emotional reactions you might have when they share something. Empathy begs it!

The valuable folks we will engage in listening might just disappoint us with an emotional attack, distasteful opinion, or personal criticism. Listen to them anyway.

If you really struggle with this, consider the "unconditional regard" I and my team practice at every callout. We have negotiated with fugitives, gang members, suspects who have tried to kill cops, and kidnappers. Regardless of any bias, we have a duty to get them out safely. This requires us to empathize with someone who might seem revolting in the cold light of day. Never mind that! We have a duty to fulfill. We don't judge. We listen with empathy. If we can do this consistently, then you can overlook the quirks of your coworkers and boss.

To show others we are empathetic, we ought to control our emotional responses to unpleasant topics or statements. These challenging statements are the stuff that trust and rapport are made of, especially if we can avoid reacting negatively and turn them into listening opportunities. This is what I mean when I say, "Listen until it hurts." If you can manage your own emotions and receive what was said and use active listening skills to respond, your relationship with that person will grow. Empathy and listening lead to trust, and trust makes conversations exponentially more fruitful.

11. RAPPORT

icebergs, minefields, & 2-faced folk

"Love all, trust a few, do wrong to none." —
William Shakespeare

Did you know that 87% of the average iceberg floats below the water's surface? That is what makes them so dangerous. The large, unseen mass of an iceberg can be devastating to unwary ship captains. The iceberg is a great metaphor for the people in our lives.

Now, I have a critical question for you. I feel like we know each other well, you and me. You've read ten chapters of this book and have not thrown it into a trash bin out of disgust! So here goes. Are you a two-faced human being cloaked in deception?

I know this seems to be a rude question to ask a new friend. Here is the truth. Everyone is "two-faced"! This sounds harsh. If you know 3,450 people, you have the same number of "faces". What I mean is that for everyone in your life, you have the part of you- your hopes, dreams, opinions, and feelings- that you freely share with that person based on the level of trust in your relationship with them. This is akin to the top part of an iceberg.

We are all like that! We must be. We treat strangers in an elevator differently than the love of our life. This is perfectly just, but it presents a problem for you as a leader of people. As a leader, you might need the buy-in of an employee, the commitment of a strategic partner, or the trust of a client. Like an iceberg, there's a huge part of that person that is hidden from you based on what they are willing to divulge. And like an iceberg, the larger portion they conceal from you could sink your ship. Great leaders learn to float the iceberg and learn more about everyone they meet. This process is called rapport building.

Rapport is the currency of leadership. Rapport refers to the trust that comes from investing in relationships. Rapport is usually built in the long-term, but professional negotiators know how to build rapport quickly using proven techniques. Hostage negotiators rely on two actions to increase rapport efficiently: actively listening to the person (Chapters 14-21) and demonstrating empathy (Chapter 10)!

Rapport is the currency of leadership.

I think of rapport in two ways. One is the short-term period of initial rapport building. Since we put on faces for strangers, initial rapport building involves breaking down defenses. A safe way to begin is by aligning common values and beliefs.

This is a delicate process. It cannot be rushed! The image you should have is from any number of old WWII movies. You have found yourself on the wrong side of a minefield! All you have is a small knife. If you remember the movies, you know the drill. Keep your cool and begin with small, probing movements. If you hit the mine, or the topic that will break trust, back up and try a different path.

We all have triggers, topics or attributes that perturb us. Some topics or statements are the equivalents of stepping on an anti-personnel mine! Do not blindly run across the field, hoping not to hit anything harmful. Listen, understand, and then proceed.

Have you ever gone to a dinner party or a tailgate at a sporting event and ran into someone new? Did you ever find that new person to be obnoxious and disagreeable? Did you ever find yourself walking away thinking the two of you were completely different? That person didn't take the time to find out what drives you! Most people are sensitive to differences. Focusing on differences is usually a death sentence for the process of building rapport.

We tend to distrust things that are different and gravitate towards people or things that we find familiar. There are biological causes for this behavior. Because of this tendency, exceptional listeners will focus on what they have in common with others. By identifying and expanding upon these similarities, leaders can build trust and buy influence on their team while still embracing diversity in human expression.

The second way I define rapport building is by describing the ideal end state. Great leaders and their teams should seek a high level of mutual disclosure. Much like a marriage, over time the partners should learn to share with each other completely. Leaders who consistently align common values and beliefs and encourage the free exchange of ideas will build trust. Trust and rapport are leadership currency. They allow leaders to build consensus, say the hard things that must be said, and influence the opinions of others. This can only happen with consistency on the part of the leader and the passage of time.

Trust earned through longitudinal rapport building creates resiliency in human relationships. This toughness allows leaders to lead and make hard decisions knowing that teams will follow. Success depends upon a culture where leaders do hard work with the support of a team! With this sort of trust relationship, leaders can manage culture using the new connections they have with their team.

Hostage negotiators obsess over rapport. We, like leaders, know that rapport is the currency that we spend to solve negotiation problems.

Hostage negotiators obsess over rapport. We, like leaders, know that rapport is the currency that we spend to solve negotiation problems. It is the wage of listening. At every crisis scene, our team has a negotiator devoted to monitoring rapport. The coach, also called the secondary negotiator, is constantly monitoring the level of rapport between the primary negotiator and the suspect. When the suspect begins to genuinely have an interest in the perspective or well-being of the negotiator, the coach detects and reports this to the team. I have learned that a peaceful surrender is not far away.

The key is to understand that trust for the sake of trust is worthless. The effort a leader puts into building rapport is best used to challenge followers to change their behavior for the better. If all you do is demonstrate empathy and build up the trust of your people, you are a therapist not a leader! If I say rapport is currency for leaders, I mean that it has real value and should be spent. We serve others as their leaders knowing we will accomplish hard work with our teams by spending our rapport to convince the team to grow and grind.

Since the analogy here is monetary, let me caution you. Effective leadership means not overspending your trust account with your team. Constantly make deposits and carefully weigh the cost of using the rapport to accomplish some task. This process of intelligently cashing in our rapport is best accomplished through "influence".

12. INFLUENCE

listening as a lever

"Every living being is an engine geared to the wheelwork of the universe. Though seemingly affected only by its immediate surrounding, the sphere of external influence extends to infinite distance."
—*Nikola Tesla*

T he very word "influence" has a negative connotation in American society. No one wants to be influenced by marketing and advertising. No one wants to be jailed for Driving Under the Influence (DUI) of alcohol or drugs. But I've got a closet full of name brand clothing I don't need and the experience of arresting hundreds of DUI drivers to show that influence can be a powerful force of motivation.

The true power of listening with empathy lies in influencing positive change. I love to ask my audience if they want to be influenced by others. Most shake their heads no. Then I ask them if they want to be influential in the lives of their children, or at work, or in their faith community. They all say yes! Influence is not a bad thing. It's high time that good people and good listeners become more influential, and bad influencers become less so. That's good leadership. That's the power of listening well.

The true power of listening with empathy lies in influencing positive change.

Influence is a process that can only begin once empathy is demonstrated and some rapport is built. Influence, for the master listener, is how tough nuts are cracked. Remember the new negotiator's mantra- "Listen until it hurts." Hostage negotiators know this well. When we are trying to help someone make a right decision, frustration can be an obstacle for the negotiation team. The solution to the crisis seems so simple for people who are not stuck in a state of crisis. Problem-solving competes with the listening process. This is my conclusion after hundreds of intense conversations where the solution seemed so simple- don't solve the problem until the problem owners are ready. And, they aren't ready until they trust you.

We usually open ourselves to the influence of other people after making a value-based judgment about their credibility. If I trust and like you, you'll have more influence over my behavior. This could be what I think, what I do, or what I buy. If you want to be influential at work, listen to people more and ask great questions. Be empathetic and earn their trust. This is the only way I've found to affect the words and deeds of others while preserving the relationship.

Influence at its best is built upon trust that comes from masterful listening. This means it rests not only upon trust, but also that empathy is the firm foundation of active listening. Now things can get interesting, because there is a clear relationship between thinking, feeling, and acting. If you can influence how someone feels or thinks, you can also influence their decisions and actions.

If you can influence how someone

*feels or thinks, you can also influence
their decisions and actions.*

If you ever wonder how hostage negotiators can broker a surrender so that everyone lives, the progression of listening-em-pathy-rapport-influence-behavior change is how we do it. This is a model used by the Federal Bureau of Investigations. It works. If we follow this guide, we become influential through the listening process to the point where the hostage taker desires to collaborate. They hand over a little bit of their agency in thinking and acting. This usually is because we intervened in how they were feeling!

Besides helping others feel good so we become influential, crisis negotiators adopt their language and create the perception we are all on the same team. With these accomplishments, negotiators can sell surrender on terms that their subjects recognize and value. What I've seen while evaluating, training, and serving with some of the finest police negotiation teams across the country and the world has caused me to believe something: what separates good from great in the crisis negotiations arena is the art of precisely developing persuasive themes.

It is in discovering what moves others that we can know how to have them subscribe to our ideas and our interests. This is a highly refined activity that requires skillful listening, inquiry, clarification, and a little intuition. These themes save lives, lead to surrenders, and sell a lot of name-brand widgets every year. Negotiators call persuasive themes "hooks", and hooks are a staple of excellent hostage and crisis negotiation teams.

One example of a common hook is the approval of a known authority. This requires us to listen and identify someone in the subject's life who is important to them. During one barricade situation, we negotiated with a woman holding her two children hostage. We learned that she revered her deceased grandmother. You might think that would not be much aid to us short of Grandma being resurrected in the Second Coming right then and there. Negotiators know better! Grandma does not have to be present or even alive to be a powerful "hook". Asking a question like, "If Grandma Bessie was here right now, what would she say?", is an excellent example of how a hook is identified and then introduced. In this case, it was effective and influential.

As a leader learns more about their followers, they can introduce themes to sell, not tell, a change in performance. This is the power of influence- to get another to do something you want them to do and have them think it was their idea in the first place!

This is the power of influence- to get another to do something you want them to do and have them think it was their idea in the first place!

Here is a message for leaders who want to be influential: be vulnerable. That is, be open to change and correction. Let your gurus, whether peers or subordinates, guide you even after you reach the top. Remember that sage counsel seldom comes from a position of formal authority. You'll have to seek it out now. Climb the mountain and sit at the feet of those who you can trust without a thought of their authority in your organizational chart. Listen well, and you'll know who is worthy of being influential in your career.

Just how can I reliably and repeatedly prove myself empathetic and trustworthy, discover how to influence others, and change human behavior while preserving valuable relationships? There are eight tools for the authentic listener. It is time to learn them. Then, you must master them.

THE 8 ACTIVE LISTENING SKILLS

CHAPTERS 13-21

13. A PREFACE TO ALS

theory becomes practice

"It's dangerous to go alone! Take this."   —
Unnamed old man with sword, The Legend of Zelda

P ay attention! This is the essential part of my book if you are
serious about becoming a better listener. First, I want this
to be an enjoyable, quick read. That was intentional. It is
not that I don't have more to say. I do! I sacrificed some of what I
would love to write to help you focus on the knowledge and skills
that best support the mission of intentional, authentic listening.
If you agree that this book is readable, I hope you will read it thor-
oughly and often. I wanted this book to provide a clear call to action and a concise system for improving your listening skillset.

Second, I want this book to be a primer for excellent listening.
This means leaders changing lives by listening authentically to
people whose stories are untold so far. To do this, you will need an
orientation to the eight active listening skills.

These eight active listening skills (ALS) work together as a
system. The system is best used to practice paying attention to
someone before selecting the most appropriate response. Each
of the techniques uses empathetic understanding and builds rapport. ALS is not an arsenal of canned responses that can be de-

ployed artificially as a script.

Do not wait to listen until a crisis develops! You are not truly listening when you whip out a list of the 8 methods and rattle them off, 1 through 8! Use ALS to improve your natural listening style.

These eight techniques are most effective when used in combination and employed covertly. An open-ended question is fantastic, but a well-designed question in conjunction with minimal encouragers and an effective pause is even better. They are so simple a cop can do them! They should be covert because we should have taken the time to make it our natural and reflexive style of inquiry and trust-building. It should not look or feel like data extraction.

Each technique is unique. They have distinct limitations and advantages. They play different roles to create an environment for storytellers to share their tales. To master listening, I believe you must become adept at each of these techniques. They are repeatable and reliable. They complement each other. I use them every day in situations both mundane and mortifying. They work in conversations with any human being with functional intelligence because they meet people right where they are. They convey empathy and build rapport. They are battle tested.

Please use them for good! Do not abuse these gifts. When I say that active listening is a skill that is the key to unlocking the universe of people, I mean it. These simple techniques rehearsed until they come naturally represent the ultimate people mover. They break down emotional resistance. Negotiators combine them with bargaining and persuasion techniques to save lives in extreme danger.

These are not parlor tricks. They are not voodoo or gimmicks. They are simple yet difficult to master. When you first begin to practice, your words will seem disjointed and unnatural. Remember that you are rewiring your brain to use a new skill. Through hard work and persistence, I promise that others will notice your new listening prowess. The bar for listening excellence is set low! For the best results, create a group of like-minded learners to provide accountability.

The listening environment is challenging. Disruptions in our systems of politics, education, faith, and industry make communications difficult. I do not send you out empty handed to lead and love. I am giving you the same toolkit that I bring with me to every life or death call out. That's how much I believe in their efficacy. Take these eight skills and never miss an opportunity to practice them!

At the end of each of the next eight chapters, you will find an added section. To make this a resource for skill-building, I have provided you with a quick review of each active listening technique. You will have at your fingertips a definition, limitations, best uses, and a few examples of the technique in action.

Most importantly, these techniques are known to us through the focus of listening practitioners like Carl Rogers who championed active listening and non-judgmental attentiveness for many years before cops realized the value of his work. My hope is that my own short extension of the work of my predecessors is worthy of this lineage!

14. ASK BETTER QUESTIONS

ALS #1: open-ended questions

"Judge a man by his questions rather than his answers." — *Voltaire*

Inquiry is the basis for all human knowledge. Discovery, examination, and experimentation have fueled an explosion in culture and technology. If you want to begin to build new skill as a listener, overhaul your usual ways of inquiry.

If you want to know more about your company and its employees, you need to ask. If you want to know more about the pretty girl or guy at the end of the bar, you'll need to inquire! In all cases, the desire to know more leads us to seek answers.

The most versatile active listening technique is to ask better questions. Some call these sorts of queries "open-ended questions". Almost exclusively, master listeners employ open-ended questions. Often, open-ended questions are described as "questions you can't answer with a yes or no", or "questions that can't be answered with a word or short phrase". Open-ended questions in these definitions are contrasted with closed-ended questions. I propose to knock down a few walls in this definition and clear the playing field for powerful inquiry.

I propose to you that open-ended questions are anything you say that invites others to tell their story! Remember the campfire? It's story-time. Just ask someone to tell a good one. When people tell you a story, you are receiving information in the way that humans have received and retained information since time began- in the form of a narrative. A good open-ended question invites the other person to tell his or her story. One of my go-to open-ended questions is no question at all. "Tell me about…", works in almost any situation where you want to know more about anyone or anything.

The key to success is a vocal tone that sells genuine curiosity not a command. My rule as a negotiator is that if I know the answer to the question and want the person to answer a certain way, it is not open-ended. If I am honestly inquiring and want the person to answer with a story that affords me new insight, then it can be a great question.

Storytelling is an ancient, sacred tradition. Human beings are made for stories, both telling and receiving. The telling of stories captures all the foundational concepts we've already explored: rapport, empathy, culture, influence, perception. Storytelling brings us together around a campfire or something just like it. Because this activity is so close to the core of how humans want to learn, there are many benefits to simply inviting people to step into the storyteller role.

Because this activity is so close to the core of how humans want to learn, there are many benefits to simply inviting people to step into the story-teller role.

One valuable benefit of asking better questions is we get critical information that otherwise would have escaped our inquiry. One of my first clients for listening training was a major general contractor. All their field supervisors had a company truck. As an exercise in asking proper open-ended questions, I started asking closed-ended data collection questions of one supervisor. Is your truck foreign or domestic? Is it a Ford, Chevy, or Dodge? Is it two-door or four? This went on to the chuckles of his colleagues for 5 minutes. Finally, I thought I knew enough about his truck to find it in the lot. I turned to his neighbor and said with an inviting tone, "Tell me about your truck." He said, "Well, first off, I'm blessed to have a take-home truck." He then gave me all the data I got from the first guy.

What just happened? How many closed-ended questions would I have to ask before I asked, "Do you feel blessed to have this truck?" Unfortunately, I would never be lucky enough to ask that. We use good questioning to invite others to tell us what they think is important. The result is that we learn what they want to tell us and in their own words. We just opened a world of discovery.

The second enormous benefit of thoughtful questioning is the discovery of our partner's preferred language. Word selection is critical for gaining insight into the mindset and motivations of our listening partners. As a negotiator, I try to interject as little of my vocabulary into the discussion as possible. The expressive words that others use offer insight into their perception. If you use words with rich personal significance, a master listener will adopt your language. Those powerful words are opportunities for rapport building if we listen for them. Until I know how you view the world and what motivates you, I cannot lead you. Your word choice will guide me as I reflect on the significance of your vocabulary and mirror these crucial words and phrases. Vocabulary is a great aid in building persuasive, influential appeals.

The most important message we send with open-ended questions is that we want to know the other person, not know things about them. We want their story, not just information. A carefully-crafted question is an invitation for a deeper understanding and a more authentic relationship.

The best open-ended questions can even break through psychological barriers to rational thought. I call these powerful inquiries "Million Dollar Questions". If I'm listening to an employee frustrated by the bureaucracy I might ask, "If you were king for a day, what would you change?" When I'm helping a suicidal subject who is convinced he needs to die today, I can ask him in all sincerity, "What's wrong with next Tuesday?" This is an opening to a discussion about the apparent (and often destructive and false) urgency they feel to act now.

I have witnessed a precisely worded question flip a figurative lever in my communication partner's mind. It works to quiet the machinery of emotion and engage the gears of logic and rational thought. If you've ever had someone exclaim, "That's a good question!" or visibly jerk to a stop, look in the distance, and begin to think, then you know the value of powerful questioning. Good questions artfully demand an answer.

Good questions artfully demand an answer.

Perhaps the purest explanation of how to harness the power of great questioning is to revert to acting like a toddler. In our toddling years, we burst onto the scene of knowledge, science, and discovery. Genuine curiosity fuels this rapid growth in intellect. Toddlers ask *why* constantly and need answers to burning questions. Leaders do well to follow their lead. Have a genuine curiosity about the people around you and the health of your organization or household. Invite people to share, and they will.

Closed-ended questions do have a narrow purpose. The only time I use a direct, yes or no or short answer question is to confirm or clarify something crucial. For gathering information, seeking understanding, relieving emotions, and conserving my energy as a listening professional, I want to ask big, open-ended questions.

Here's a simple example. If I witness an employee violate a key policy at work, the temptation would be to immediately tell the employee that they violated a policy and counsel them about this infraction and document it in their file. What if instead of jumping right to a finding of fact (violation of policy) and discipline, we instead asked a few open-ended questions? One great question would be, "I noticed you did this. Why did you do it that way?" When I work with managers, they tell me they might lose authority when they ask why. Instead, might we better understand what went wrong in process of training this employee to follow the policy? Might we discover this is a broader problem than one employee or that our training needs revising because it is unclear?

Never in the history of calming down has anyone ever calmed down by a person of authority merely ordering them to calm down. An advanced application of open-ended questions could be the best method I've found to get people "thinking well" instead of feeling bad. The hypothetical open-ended question shows off this technique's versatility. "What if..." questions are powerful tools when employed with finesse.

Never in the history of calming down has anyone ever calmed down by a person of authority merely ordering them to calm down.

When people are emotional and frustrated with your authority as a parent, manager, hostage negotiator, or leader, then this can work. Just ask what they would do if they were in charge! Let them explore the consequences of choosing what they want even if this is self-destructive or hurtful to others. In the process, they are compelled to use their rational brain. They vent their negative emotions and will tell you much about their mindset and ability to bargain. When the time is right, you can gently take back the reins of the conversation and I've always found they are calmer, friendlier, and more reasonable.

Recently, my ten-year old son, Ray, didn't want to go to bed on a school night. This is how it went:

Me: "Ray, it's time to go to bed."

Ray: "I don't want to. I'm not going!"

Me: "If you were the dad, what time would you make you go to bed?"

Ray: "I wouldn't go to bed."

Me: "OK. What would you do the next morning if you were the dad and you were grumpy and didn't want to get up for school?"

Ray: "I wouldn't make me get up."

Me: "What if you didn't want to go to school the next day either?"

Ray: "No school."

Me: "And what would you do if you were the dad and you didn't go to school for so long and couldn't go on to the next grade?"

Ray: ... "I don't know." (With each question, Ray became less emotional and more thoughtful. The vocal tone was now conversational.)

Me: "Well, since I'm the real dad, and we don't want to be in 5th Grade forever, please go to bed."

Ray: "Okay, Dad." (He surrendered!)

Great questions are not just for getting answers. Used with precision, the right questions can help break someone out of an emotional state. Ray needed his rational brain to imagine being me. With each question that required the hypothetical role-play, Ray got calmer and more rational. His insistence on staying up was tied to his emotions about not having to go to bed. As with most parenting problems, he was tired! Instead of arguing back and forth, or telling him to calm down, a simple line of questioning accomplishes everything we need to negotiate a surrender. It doesn't just work on my awesome son Ray or on 10-year old boys. Hostage negotiators use it all the time!

"What if..." questions are powerful tools when employed with finesse.

Begin your listening journey by intentionally constructing

better questions. Give people space to think and then respond. At all times, control your tone and have an earnest spirit of inquiry. Don't ask gotcha questions or advocate for one answer or another. If you ask a question to get your preferred answer, don't be surprised if empathy and rapport evaporate. It's not about you. Listen well because the story is theirs!

❊ ❊ ❊

ALS NAME:
Open-ended Questions

DEFINITION:
Anything you say that invites someone to tell his or her story.

USES:
Gathering better information;
Diminishing the listener's control of the teller's story;
Emphasizing the word choice of the subject;
Allowing the subject to vent;
Using hypothetical questions to switch someone from emotional to rational;
Creating perception in the subject's mind that we are listening as they do most of the talking;
Efficiently moving to story-telling, not data collection.

LIMITATIONS:
Combine with use of other techniques to show a deeper understanding. Can seem like we are controlling the narrative if we asktoo many questions without other listening techniques.

EXAMPLE(S):
Any question that starts with What, Who, Where, How, or When is a good start. Avoid "Can you tell me…?" and "Do you…?" as these are surefire closed-ended questions.

Be careful with "Why?" questions, as people in emotional crisis might interpret this as being judgmental if you don't sell it with an empathetic voice. Use "How come?" as a safe alternative.

Questions using "imagine", "if", and "what if" can be powerful ofr painting vision and conducting discovery while avoiding negative emotional reactions.

Try instead:
"What happened tonight to bring us here?"
"Please tell me what happened."
"If you were in charge, what would you do?"
"How did this happen?"

15. REWARDING STORYTELLERS

ALS #2: minimal encouragers

"Rudy! Rudy! Rudy!"
—The Notre Dame faithful on November 8, 1975

One of the greatest fears human beings report having is a fear of public speaking. They fear public speaking even more than death! I'm a public speaker, and I have some insight into this common fear. I still get butterflies when I walk on to the stage. Despite this fear, I keep at it because I'm after my fix!

No one fears public speaking when they nail a gig. My goal as a speaker is to evoke the kind of emotional engagement that Rudy Rutiger's teammates had at the end of the movie when they carry him off the field past Touchdown Jesus. That sort of public speaking performance rewards the brain just like cocaine! No one fears that sort of joyful success that comes from a stadium chanting your name.

What we do fear is having the audience loathe us. We are anxious about the possibility that our audience may react by carrying us, not past Touchdown Jesus in Rudy, but out of town on a rail to be thrown in the river as in *O Brother Where Art Thou?* I have come to believe that this fear is not just for formal speeches on a stage. Anyone sharing that story of self also risks the rejection of their dearly held message.

Audiences have the power to invalidate the story and the storyteller. This might be why great ideas and powerful narratives lurk in the shadows. Master listeners must create the campfire culture and coax speakers out to sit on the stumps! When we do, we relieve the natural fear that speakers have.

Negotiators are often faced with tense circumstances in our barricades and hostage crises. We learn to anticipate hours and hours of listening and bargaining with emotionally unstable actors. We favor techniques that conserve energy. For this reason, hostage negotiators are trained to use "minimal encouragers".

People need encouragement. We use non-verbal and para-verbal communication, and short, positive, verbal communication to demonstrate we are listening and appreciate what is being said. Try it! Smile, nod affirmatively, keep your body posture open and inviting, and use remarks like "yes", "I see", "right", and "great!" Do these simple things with great sincerity, and it is like holding a cue card that says, "Tell me more!"

After learning and using minimal encouragers for years, it struck me why they work so well. These simple gestures speak directly to everyone's fear of rejection and invalidation. They reassure our speaker that we are listening, we like what we hear, and we want to hear more of this story!

These simple gestures speak directly to everyone's fear of rejection and invalidation.

What are minimal encouragers? They are a spoken word or phrase, posture, gesture, or action that reassures the speaker and encourages them to continue the story. All the ALS techniques I share with you require an empathetic tone that matches the intensity of the conversation. Minimal encouragers are sold with your voice and body!

Minimal encouragers begin with orienting our posture towards our speaker. We create the impression that they are the most important person at that moment. We can signal to them that their message is the most important thing in our environment and it has captured our attention. Maintaining eye contact, nodding, smiling, facing them, opening our posture by uncrossing arms, and leaning in are all subconscious signs of "paying attention" and being "open" to receive the message.

Even more encouraging are words of agreement and positive regard. Saying "OK!", "good", "yes", and "I agree" show them we are listening and want them to keep speaking. They can be said even while the person speaks if said without deliberation and in a softer tone and lower volume. This takes some practice, but it is simple and effective. Minimal encouragers can be used when the person sharing their story pauses to indicate we are listening and they should keep going.

A powerful application of this technique can be used when they tell us something profound, sad, or disheartening. I have used it for years as a negotiator and it seals rapport firmly. With the right tone, simply reply, "Wow." The sort of "wow" that shows you recognize the gravity of what she just said. In one word with a minimum of energy in setting the proper tone, you show you are listening well and understand without saying two of the most dreaded words I don't want to hear from the mouth of a police negotiator in training: "I understand." Don't say this. If you want to convey that you understand, use an ALS technique! Saying "I understand" is not a minimal encourager. It is an invitation to argue with an angry person. People and their traumas are complex! It would take a long time to truly understand them, and even longer to prove to them that you do. Use minimal encouragers to show you are listening and set up opportunities for the other ALS tools to show what you understand and foster more storytelling.

There's a bonus to using minimal encouragers. How much energy does it take to use this technique? Almost none. If you struggle with being empathetic because you tend to dominate conversations through interrupting or one-upping, minimal encouragers by design force you to let others speak their mind. In the process, you can save your emotional energy for the other techniques in the ALS family.

Minimal encouragers are the perfect complement to the other techniques, but they don't come without risk. Since the technique is a simple and shallow skill compared to the others, it should not be the sole method of actively listening. If it is overused, it can be distracting to the speaker. Perhaps most importantly, the tone of voice for spoken encouragers is critical to show authenticity.

Minimal encouragers are the perfect complement to the other techniques, but they don't come without risk.

When used appropriately and in combination with the other ALS skills, they speak directly to the need for a listener to be and appear to be attentive. Words and voice are powerful, but they cannot overcome the language of our body, especially our facial expressions. Match all three and send a clear signal that you are open for masterful listening. You are an audience of one, so reward your speaker!

❋ ❋ ❋

ALS NAME:
Minimal encouragers

DEFINITION:
Small gestures or a few words used to demonstrate appreciation for the speaker and encourage them to continue their story.

USES:
Conserve energy;

Relieve anxiety in the speaker;
Emphasize the word choice of the subject;
Create perception in the subject's mind that we are listening as they do most of the talking;
Efficiently extend the storytelling.

LIMITATIONS:
Requires use of other techniques to show a deeper understanding.
Can be overused and are risky if you don't sell the words with your tone of voice.

EXAMPLE(S):
Eye contact.
Orienting your body towards the speaker
Using an open posture by uncrossing arms.
Eliminating environmental distractions; ignore computers, phones, watches, clocks, et al.
Nodding and smiling.
"Yes."
"OK."
"I agree."
"Wow!"
"Whoa!"
Use of a curious, surprised, confused, or agreeable tone of voice.

16. TAMING EMOTIONS

ALS #3: emotion labeling

"The best and most beautiful things in the world cannot be seen or even touched. They must be felt with the heart."
—Helen Keller

Human emotions fuel crisis. As a crisis negotiator, I am sent to high-risk incidents where police officers without specialized training and experience can't manage the chaos. In almost every case, intensely negative human emotions form a barrier to productivity and peace.

With all the conflict that comes out of emotional distress, it is easy to think emotions are the enemy. When I became a manager of people, I sometimes wished they weren't so emotional. When I present my workshops to managers of people in all sorts of industries, they agree! It is tempting to demand that our employees refrain from bringing emotions to work. This ignores a simple fact: human beings are emotional creatures!

It is tempting to demand that our employees

> *refrain from bringing emotions to work. This ignores a simple fact: human beings are emotional creatures!*

Suppose I had the power to completely remove all human emotions from a work environment. Would this be a place free of drama? Would employees become more productive? Would everyone be satisfied and engaged? I am convinced that no one would choose to come to a workplace devoid of emotion.

We need our emotions. In a strong sense, we ARE our emotions. We are emotional creatures. Joy is a foundational feature of a vibrant workplace. Passion for the work is a key ingredient in a desirable job. If you remove all emotion, you lose the reasons most people stay engaged in their work. Moreover, once you've progressed in your listening journey a short way, you'll begin to see "negative" human emotions as opportunities to tighten the bonds of your relationship. We need great listener-leaders precisely when our emotions sour from grief, sadness, or discouragement. Here's an important and often overlooked truth. Strong, negative emotions are communication. When the emotional brain is in control, the person is trying to tell us something important. Smart leaders listen and address the emotions as they arise.

Here is the challenge of leading people who have honest emotions: it seems like the solution is to remove all emotion from the workplace. This is not correct. We do not want an emotionless environment at work. The task is much harder. We want to select which emotions we encourage at work. This represents a challenge for leaders. We need a reliable method to relieve negative emotions and amplify positive emotions.

> *This represents a challenge for leaders. We need a reliable method to relieve negative emotions and amplify positive emotions.*

Negative emotions are those that make it harder for employees to work well. Fear, anxiety, depression, anger, distrust, frustration, disappointment, jealousy, and envy top the list of the types of emotion that inhibit fruitful work. Everyone has bad days. We all have experienced these troubling emotions. Give thanks for this gift! This common human experience of emotions is what allows a leader to recognize and empathize with each member of their team.

If you want to be a master listener, accept the fact that emotions are real. How we feel impacts what we think and how we act. Our feelings are not evil or atrocious. They just are. Negative emotions are an opportunity for a skilled listener to intervene. Negative emotions and their causes are opportunities in a listening situation. Talking about these emotions is a proven method to build trust.

It is the duty of managers of people to be on the lookout for negative emotions. If an employee seems to be having a bad day, it's the manager's mission to let the employee know that this emotion is apparent to the manager.

Without being accusatory and without stating it as a fact, a master listener can make an observation like, "It seems like you are sad today." Even without asking it in the form of a question, this statement is an invitation to the sad employee for them to agree and explain why or disagree and clarify their mood. This is called labeling the emotion. It is a powerful active listening skill. Anytime emotions are impeding the resolution of a crisis, a trained negotiator will use this technique. The negotiator will continue to label any negative emotions as they appear.

A good emotion label with the agreement of the one exhibiting the emotion causes something magical to occur. The power of the negative emotion over that person diminishes! Perhaps it is because we spend so much time trying to let others know how we are feeling without saying anything. Perhaps it is because it is a calming effect when someone understands our mood. All I know is that this consistently and reliably works.

In a customer service environment, labeling emotions is a requirement to successfully defuse a client's awful experience. You can even shortcut the process. Anyone who had a bad experience with the products or services your organization provides will be angry, disappointed, frustrated, or some combination of those three.

Let the client know you recognize these emotions when you see or hear them! In many cases, that is why they called or walked in to complain. With that vital task out of the way, it is common for the emotions to melt away. Then the problem can be solved rapidly. Most of the time, the problem has already been corrected; the purpose of the complaint was simply to communicate the ill feeling the customer experienced.

Avoid problem-solving until you've addressed all negative emotions with a good label and their agreement. Master listeners don't waste time solving a problem until they've listened to understand the core problem, its causes, and built the trust necessary to work with the problem's owner to find the right fix. This requires labeling and relieving negative emotions. Fail to acknowledge the emotion and watch the person resist any attempt at problem solving! Attacking the emotional problem first is the most efficient route to a happy customer.

Master listeners don't waste time solving a problem until they've listened to understand the core problem, its causes, and built the trust necessary to work with the problem's owner to find the right fix.

The emotion label is not just for negative emotions! Great listeners and confident managers can label positive emotions. If someone is having a great day, acknowledge that! "You look joyful!" There's more magic here. When we label a positive emotion and the other person agrees, the positive emotion amplifies. Try it. In all cases, when you find human emotion, do not ignore it.

Label it. Find agreement. Watch for the change. Bad emotions will recede, and good emotions will advance. Now we can use other listening techniques with more impact.

On the wall of the FBI Crisis Negotiation Unit headquarters in Quantico, Virginia, there is a simple poster of a large donut shape. The ring of the pastry is “Emotions” and the donut hole is labelled “The Story”. The FBI knows that learning the facts and circumstances of someone’s story is important. They also know that discovering the emotions wrapped around the story is necessary. You don’t really know the story until you know how they feel.

When we as leaders ignore emotions, we lose the trust of our followers and miss the point of their stories. If you want a healthy culture, manage the emotions of the workplace. Your people are watching. When you shirk a duty as important as making people feel good about coming to work, how can you expect them to trust you? For a handy aid in mastering emotions as a listening leader, check out the quick reference guide at the end of this book!

* * *

ALS NAME:
Emotion labeling

DEFINITION:
Recognizing an emotion and making this observation knownto the owner of the emotion.

USES:
Calming negative emotions;
Amplifying positive emotions;
Demonstrating empathy and emotional understanding called "attunement";
Inviting dialogue about the causes of emotions;
Providing excellent customer service.

LIMITATIONS:

Should be formatted properly- non-accusatory and in the form of an observation. Best used when an emotion is obvious. The name we describe the emotion with MUST make sense to them and be an emotion/name they are willing to agree with. Be precise. The closer you can get to the specific emotion, the greater the impact. Avoid vague terms like "upset" or "emotional".

EXAMPLE(S):

"You seem angry."

"It sounds like you are depressed."

"I can see that you are having a great day!"

17. SOMETIMES SAY NOTHING

ALS #4: effective pauses

"Silence is better than unmeaning words."   —
Pythagoras

As a professional speaker, it may seem ironic for me to write about saying nothing. I have never gotten smarter while speaking. I learn a lot at my keynotes. For me, learning comes after I speak as I am asked insightful questions during the "mandatory" Q and A session I build into most of my events. More learning comes during the post-speech feedback in person, via e-mail, or over the internet on LinkedIn. The adage remains that God gave us one mouth and two ears- so communicate accordingly! Sometimes, good listening means not talking.

Effective pauses are an active listening technique designed to elicit crucial information from our communication partners. They are pauses made to create silence. Effective pauses work best when they are intentional and strategic. The beauty of a well-designed effective pause is that it demonstrates respect and empathy to the other person. Effective pauses require discipline on the part of a skilled listener. The payoff from a perfectly timed pause is incredible because pauses work in so many situations.

Fear is a powerful motivator. For this reason, fear is also a powerful de-motivator. Many of your best employees, clients, and loved ones are afraid to tell you the truth. Out of fear of reprisal, hurt feelings, or a nasty argument, we bite our tongue most of the time. This reluctance to speak can kill companies. It contributes to the isolation that leaders can experience. Leaders who don't listen, or who make a habit of killing messengers, become insulated from reality because everyone in the organization is reluctant to tell them the truth. This phenomenon is not new. "The Emperor's new clothes are fabulous!" should sound familiar.

Somehow in some way, as a master listener, I must convince everyone that they can tell me the truth no matter how much it hurts. If I can capture this feedback and these tough truths, I can exponentially improve myself, my team, and any mission on my plate. Providing a quiet space for reflection can make all the difference.

Effective pauses are so powerful that they can be used in extreme situations. To quote my colorful Aunt Tabitha, "People are funny creatures. An octopus squirts ink out of its 'rear', but people lie." Good listeners know how to use effective pauses to deal with deception and outright lies.

As a hostage negotiator, I always begin with a deficit in trust. I work with total strangers, which means I have no rapport bank from which to make withdrawals. Many of these strangers have a rich pattern of interaction with the police and do not trust me as a member of law enforcement. I must make substantial efforts to build rapport before I can create any influential leverage. Often, I'm dealing with a mentally-ill subject with exhibiting paranoia. Sometimes I am speaking with a suicidal person who is afraid to tell me about their desire for self-harm. This can be because they are afraid of stigma. They worry that I will think they are crazy, or they do not want me to try to stop them. Sometimes, I am on the phone with a criminal who doesn't want to go to prison. In all these cases, there are real motivations for the other person to conceal the truth.

Good listeners know how to use effective pauses to deal with deception and outright lies.

Aren't you glad that you don't have to worry about your colleagues failing to tell you something critical for the success of your project? And isn't it great to know they would never lie to you about something important? And it's certainly a warm fuzzy for us all since our employees always come to us at the first sign of a mistake, right? You and I know that all the questions in this paragraph are based upon false assumptions.

What a shame. It's scary to think how much information we miss because people are afraid, reluctant to speak, or maliciously concealing the truth. That's where effective pauses come in.

Remember our campfire? What good would it do to stoke the fire, arrange the chairs, sit down with our friends, and then barrage them with questions and unsolicited opinions? Great listening often comes down to not only know just what to say and when to say it, but in the case of this effective pause whether to say anything at all.

Another name for an effective pause might be "wait-time". Demonstrating empathy means I'm not trying to control the conversation. Practicing wait-time helps reduce the poor listening habit of interrupting. It's as simple as waiting for 5 MISSISSIPPIs after your fellow communicator stops speaking. Here's what happens in those five seconds. Your partner is watching your reaction. You have a warm, open posture and are still being attentive. They begin wondering if you aren't listening, but there you are, visibly engaged. They then begin wondering if they didn't make it clear that they were done. And they also remember one or two important things they wanted to tell you. The silence grows and grows. The silence is unbearable, so they add the things they forgot and just keep on talking!

If you want to master this tool, you must be comfortable with silence. When I was in the Roman Catholic seminary, I went on a three-day silent retreat. For 72 hours, there was no conversation or electronics in our seminary. That was my first experience with intentional silence. It was unnerving.

Silence creates a physiological space since no sound reaches your ear. Silence also creates a social void. Silence is so rare in society that the pause in a conversation causes us to think, "Someone should say something!" If we are having a conversation and suddenly neither one of us is talking, it feels awkward. The longer the silence the more awkward the feeling! Eventually, it seems that we are both violating a social norm that requires us to speak. As a skilled listener, I should embrace this awkwardness and know that good will come from it.

If your storyteller is reluctant, using wait time when they speak gives them the sense that you are not in a rush to tell your own story and are not going to interrupt. It presents to them an image of you as a thoughtful and receptive listener. They already feel listened to!

If your storyteller is being deceptive, a thoughtful and engaged communication partner seems more likely to see through the smokescreen of the lie. It creates a perception of risk for the deceiver. As a criminal interviewer for fifteen years, I learned to use an intentional pause whenever someone told me a whopper. Instead of creating a confrontation, the silence creates pressure. The anxiety from telling a lie grows as the lie was the last thing said and it lingers! Many times, the deception wilts and they will walk back the deception, explain more, soften the lie, or change the subject.

The best way to become a competent user of "wait-time" as a listening technique is to get intentional silence every day. Consider it your listening vitamin. Once a day, get 30 minutes of intentional silence. This is not a self-help pop-psych manual, so I'll spare you the research to support the case for intentional silence to aid your physical and mental well-being. Better listening should be all the reason you need.

> *The best way to become a competent user
> of "wait-time" as a listening technique is
> to get intentional silence every day.*

I get mine during my commute. No cell phone, no radio, no talking- just drive and think. If you surround yourself with noise to feel at ease, using effective pauses will be a major challenge at first. Work on it. Effective pauses are versatile. They work to let people expound upon a good story, to encourage someone gathering their thoughts in crisis, and to break through deception. When you recognize false statements, resist the temptation to take it personally. Lies tell us as much as the truth in most cases. You know what is true and that they are not comfortable with that truth.

There is emotional content in deception, so consider the use of an emotion label or a paraphrase or reflection, (you'll learn about these in the next few chapters). In the same vein, take a deep breath and pause when your storyteller makes their story a direct attack or outlandish accusation. You have several options with ALS when someone makes it personal. One viable option is to use an effective pause. It is the classic refusal to dignify the offensive remark with a response. The break in the action can draw out more of the cause for the outburst or allow the offender to reflect on the inappropriate nature of what he said.

Sometimes, my clients ask why these effective pauses work so well even in regular conversations with no deception in play. I've come to understand that they work so well across all our relationships because they give respect. Pausing and waiting in silence gives people space to speak their mind. The key to a good pause is that it is intentional: you have in your mind that this is the right time to simply give the other person the space to speak. You must be committed. Particularly in the case of someone afraid to speak, their reluctance will require you to steel yourself against the temptation to blurt something out to erase the awkward feeling. While you wait, use nonverbal minimal encouragers!

There might also be a peculiar benefit to some effective pauses in intense situations. This is part of the "magic" of listening well. For some reason, when confronted with that awkwardness, the rational brain defers to the emotional brain, and your communications partner may blurt out something they did not want to reveal. I think sometimes the emotional brain is so desperate to break the silence, it will grab the first words it finds in your mind. Often, those very words the rational brain was thinking about NOT saying. Again, I don't understand why the magic works sometimes. I've seen it occur in real life negotiations enough to anticipate this oddity before it happens.

❋ ❋ ❋

ALS NAME:
Effective pauses

DEFINITION:
Silence with a purpose.

USES:
Gathering better information;
Giving someone space and time to think of a response;
Demonstrates respect;
Prevents you, the listener from interjecting emotion;
Highlights their lousy behavior or emotionally offensive speech;
Encourages them to continue their line of storytelling.

LIMITATIONS:
Must be used at an appropriate time. Requires commitment and intention. Can be overused. Be ready to reassure them you are listening- you just wanted to let them finish or have time to think of the best answer.

EXAMPLE(S):

Silence when they pause in speaking if you believe they have more to say.

Silence when they say or do something harmful to the dialogue; i.e. call you a name, tell a lie, or make an outlandish accusation.

Silence after you ask a question that deserves an answer.

18. POWERFUL WORDS

ALS #5: reflecting

"Language is the armory of the human mind, and at once contains the trophies of its past and the weapons of its future conquests."   *—Samuel Taylor Coleridge*

T he words we choose tell others a lot about us. How I see the world becomes apparent in my vocabulary. Master listeners can adopt the language of another to connect with them on a deeper level. The active listening technique that carefully searches for keywords is called reflecting. Reflecting is often set up for success with great open-ended questions. The better the question, the more potential there is for our communication partners to use the sort of words negotiators love to reflect upon!

Reflecting is simple. It is the process of recognizing significant words that other people use. By merely repeating these words back in the form of a question, a master listener can encourage the speaker to explain the meaning or importance of these key terms. This active listening technique is the equivalent of plucking the choice fruit from the orchard tree. Word selection offers excellent insight into intellectual perspectives, beliefs, values, motivations, and intention.

Intellectual perspective is a fancy term that describes "how we see the world". If I think that everything is meant to be and there are no coincidences, then you may need to change your mindset to craft a persuasive theme for me. If I think that everything I do is meaningless, you will want to know that before you try to help me solve a problem! These sorts of worldviews become apparent when we listen to the language of others.

Reflecting as a listening tactic is adept at "unpacking" all the important things. Listen to my words, and you will know what I think is true or false. Now you know what I believe. Listen to what I like and dislike and you will know my values. When I use complex terms, listen carefully. Every dense word that could have multiple meanings should be explored.

When listening to the valuable people in your life, ask them to explain what they meant when they said these powerful words. In my experience, everyone is their own favorite subject. The master listener becomes conversant in the subject of another's views by understanding these crucial words and concepts. People trust those who can speak their language accurately.

---

*People trust those who can speak
their language accurately.*

Reflecting is useful to prevent misunderstanding. It is not parroting. We use this technique to discover the meaning of words, not to blindly repeat them hoping our definition matches theirs.

Another application of this principle is handy when the conversation is intense, or we are overwhelmed by the pace or tone of the conversation. A simple tactic can help you get your bearings and slow down the pace of the conversation. Reflecting used this way can be called mirroring. In this usage, we are simply holding a mirror up to the last word or phrase they said. We just add a question mark using our inflection. Now we have invited further dialogue using their own words and making them into a question. It is a cruder technique since we are not analyzing the conversation to find the key words like in the first application in the reflecting method. By mirroring, we are playing verbal ping pong and returning the last word or phrase to buy us time to get into our active listening groove.

The real value of effective reflecting is found in the identification of significant vocabulary that reveals so much about the other person. With this technique, a master listener can quickly discover the speaker's world view. Police crisis negotiators listen to identify:

- Beliefs
- Values
- Motivations
- Fears
- Perceived obstacles to surrender, especially past trauma
- Hopes
- Aspirations

We do this by analyzing the words people use and reflecting these terms to invite them to explain. When they take us up on this invitation and detail these concepts, we learn all we need to know to craft persuasive appeals. We can adopt these words as our own when the other person explains their meaning and import. Reflecting the language of our listening partner is a tremendous aid in building rapport.

ALS NAME:
Reflecting

DEFINITION:
Inquiring about significant words in the story to invite explan-

ation.

USES:
Control the pace;
Identify values, beliefs, perspectives, intentions, and motivations;
Building rapport;
Creating perception in the subject's mind that we are listening as they do most of the talking;
Discovering language that we can adopt for persuasion.

LIMITATIONS:
You will develop an ear for the proper words to reflect. The more complex and emotional the word is, the more fertile the reflection. Must be sold with the tone of voice that assures you are sincerely inquiring. Careful to NOT reflect with a tone of sarcasm or to choose a word that is caustic. Don't reflect too many times in a row or too frequently. It becomes an obstacle because it seems like a trick.

EXAMPLE(S):
Storyteller: "The situation is hopeless! Everything I've tried has failed!"
Master Listener: "Failed?" or "Hopeless?" tone: surprised

Storyteller: "I can't go on."
Master Listener: "Go on?" tone: curious

Storyteller: "Sometimes when I'm driving to this place, I realize I've been working here 20 years with nothing to show for it."
Master Listener: "20 years." tone: agreement
Storyteller: "Yeah! That's a long time, isn't it?!"

19. INSIGHTFUL LISTENING

ALS #6. paraphrasing

"No law or ordinance is mightier than understanding."
—Plato

L istening is a deep dive into empathy. Genuinely seeking the perspective of another person requires the master listener to reflect significant words, label emotions, and ask great questions. Now, consider what your listening partners will think when you *hear* the words they *don't* say. Most of us fail to adequately express the thoughts, aspirations, ideas, and concepts we want to share with others. We are constantly searching for the right words to connect with clients, prospects, bosses, peers, family, and even friends. Add in some negative emotions or a confusing environment, and this desperate attempt to be understood is even more challenging.

Hidden in the words they choose and wrapped in their emotions, I often find the main idea my clients are trying to convey. This is the "moral of the story" we all want to tell. This is what a listener must recognize if he or she is committed to the craft.

The art of hearing the unspoken truth in the story is the potent active listening technique called paraphrasing. While reflecting repeats a word spoken by our listening partner, paraphrasing means extracting the words that best capture the main idea of the communication we receive. We make a simple observation about the speaker and their message and await confirmation or clarification.

Here is an example. I was summoned to a negotiation with a teenage boy. He was drunk and broke into his ex-girlfriend's apartment looking for her. Fortunately, she was not home, so his rash decision turned into a barricade call for our SWAT team. I talked with him for hours. I listened as he complained about the failed relationship and his hopelessness. I said, "It sounds like you can't see a future without her." He never said those words. I just recognized that is what he was trying to tell me, a total stranger until just a few hours before. It opened a new portal into his world and earned rapport we desperately needed.

Telling these intimate truths is hard work! Be patient. Disclosing important truths often leaves people at a loss for the perfect words. By listening well, we can show that we get the point and help them cut to the heart of their story. Now we've done them a great service.

By listening well, we can show that we get the point and help them cut to the heart of their story. Now we've done them a great service.

Paraphrasing is a wonderful tool for managing the tone of a conversation. Often, my negotiation partner is angry and verbally abusive. When they lace their message with profanity, aggressive language, or personal attacks, I use paraphrasing with a twist.

This application of paraphrasing can be called "soften and rephrase" when the other person is using negative, emotional language. I can delete the offensive words and tone and replace it with something more constructive. "All you f***ing cops should f***ing leave!!! You're f***ing p***ing me off! I can't think straight!" when paraphrased, becomes "It sounds like you want us to move farther away so you have more room to think." Not the subject's words, but his message packaged constructively. That is how to paraphrase like a professional!

Clarification is another benefit of seeking the main idea. You can help someone, in crisis or just having a regular Tuesday afternoon, to better understand their own values, beliefs, and desires. Paraphrasing used as clarification might use questions like, "I think you mean this ___. Am I right?" Or, "Do you mean ___?"

Now I want to let you in on a fantastic and often overlooked capability of paraphrasing. People want to be understood. In crisis, this desire becomes intense. You just learned in an earlier chapter that in my years of negotiating, a phrase I have learned to avoid is "I understand". Saying you understand usually means you don't. People and their crises are so complex, that understanding them is rare. In crisis mode, many people reject this statement and challenge whether you understand at all. Instead, paraphrase and prove to them you understand *before* they ever ask if you do. When you pick up on the hidden messages of motivation, value, and belief there is no doubt that you are attuned to your subject.

ALS NAME:
Paraphrasing

DEFINITION:
Offering insights that are unspoken but true.

USES:
Demonstrate understanding;
Clarify values, beliefs, perspectives, intentions, and motivations;
Building rapport;
Helping them organize their thoughts and words;
Inviting deeper dialogue;

Test-driving themes for persuasion and influence.

LIMITATIONS:
It is risky to ask if something is true that has not been stated yet. Must be sold with the tone of voice that assures you are sincerely inquiring.

EXAMPLE(S):
Storyteller: "My uncle isn't answering his phone! I don't know what to do! I need to talk to him.

Master Listener: "It sounds like your uncle is important to you."

Storyteller: "You cops are all the same. You never mind your own business. You make me crazy!"

Master Listener: "It sounds like you've had some bad experiences with the police."

20. THE RUN DOWN

ALS #7. summarizing

"Of emotions, of love, of breakup, of love and hate and death and dying, mama, apple pie, and the whole thing. It covers a lot of territory, country music does." —Johnny Cash

Humans are funny creatures. I negotiate with a huge swath of humanity. Each person has different appearances and personalities, frailties and triggers. Despite all their differences, I can predict one consistent occurrence in these intense conversations. Early on, each of them will challenge me with some variation of this question- "Are you really listening?"

This is a dangerous question! My readers who are married have probably heard this query before. If we failed at this challenge, we probably did so by repeating the last phrase we heard. The tailor-made response to anyone who questions your listening authenticity is a summary. This is not regurgitation or a simple mirroring technique. A proper summary captures all the main ideas or events that the speaker spoke to us. Then we add in the emotion that is most prevalent in the story.

Recall that the excellent negotiators with FBI Crisis Negotiation Unit in Quantico, Virginia know to focus on the "story donut". This is their belief that a great story will always be wrapped up in both the story itself and the emotions that come with it. It's not enough to get the facts or the emotions. You need both! I happen to think they are exactly right. That's the power of a great summary.

If you can remember the main ideas and the emotion, few people will doubt that you are a master listener. Summaries are useful in other applications. They can be used as a pivot in a conversation. If you want to move in a different direction with your questions or their response, use a summary to ensure you've understood what has been said so far and to bring the earlier line of thought to a satisfying conclusion.

For this reason, summarizing is useful to end conversations too! Although no one likes to be interrupted, cut off, or ejected from your office, there's a loophole for a summary. People *do* like to hear their own words repeated and to know that you were listening. A summary can be a pleasant way to make an excuse to end the discussion and close the conversation for the moment while sealing rapport.

A summary can be a pleasant way to make an excuse to end the discussion and end the conversation while sealing rapport.

One additional use of the summary technique is to control the pace of a conversation. If our speaker is excited and speaking too quickly for them to think, we need a way to interrupt without offending her. We need a kind way to slow the pace down so we can listen better. Summarize! I've faithfully used this on the street as a patrol officer and sergeant for years. I interrupt them without apology by saying, "WAIT, WAIT, WAIT! Are you saying - A, B, C- and you're angry about this?" I begin speaking loudly and rapidly to match the speaker's original pace, but by the end of the summary I've slowed down, softened my tone, and lowered my volume. I do this to draw their attention and seek their confirmation or clarification.

I also do this because of the psychological principle of pacing. By moving the dials for pace, tone, and volume, I often see my partner match these aspects with their voice. It's more than a parlor trick. It is a kindness to offer emotional people the chance to gather their words. When they regain control of their voice, they also tend to think more clearly because they have regained some control of their rational mind.

Each of these listening techniques has a unique range of applications. Each has limitations in employment and unique abilities in eliciting another person's story. Summarizing is not a great way to begin since you won't have all the best selections of ideas and emotions. Johnny Cash might have summarized all of country music in this chapter's epigraph, but he had a deep dive into the history of the genre. You will want some exposure to what your listening partner is going through to pull off an epic summary like Mr. Cash.

Once you have listened enough to have the major developments and emotions, summarizing has the capability to seal trust and prove that you are actively listening. It can control the flow of the conversation and end conversations without ending a relationship. Such versatility makes the summary statement a powerful companion in your journey to masterful listening.

ALS NAME:
Summarizing

DEFINITION:
3 Paraphrasing + Emotion Labeling; a recap of the critical discoveries of a listening session.

USES:
Control the pace and direction of the conversation;

Get out of unproductive listening sessions when crunched for time;
Demonstrate understanding;
Interrupt, in a good way;
Seal rapport;
Prove you were listening when challenged;
Induce THEM to listen to YOU;
Transition to problem-solving.

LIMITATIONS:
Only as good as what you've remembered about emotions, themes, and key concepts they have divulged.

EXAMPLE(S):
Storyteller: "Are you even listening to me?!"
Master Listener: "I hope so. Let me see if I got this right? Your wife left you Wednesday, your dog ran away Friday, and you had to drive in your pickup truck in the rain to the train station to pick up Grandma on Saturday. And this makes you sad."

Master Listener: "Hang on! Are you saying...1...2...3? What did I miss?"

21. SENDING THE MESSAGE

ALS #8. "I"-Messages

"You must reward the kind of behavior you want."
—*General James Mattis, USMC (Ret.)*

T he last active listening skill requires precision. All the rest give a lot of room for personal style and tailoring to circumstances. Not the "I"-Message. This final technique for listening well must be strictly constructed. Here's the format:

"I (my emotion) when you (your behavior), because (reason)".

These three elements must be in this order or the technique is all but doomed.

The "I"-Message is high-risk, high-reward. Pick the right point in the listening opportunity and construct it with care, and the "I"-Message is unparalleled in putting boundaries around bad behavior and reinforcing behavior that helps.

This method of discussing someone's behavior is useful because it is framed in the context of my emotions- a topic that for almost everyone is off limits. People will argue all day about their behavior and its moral quality, but to argue with the listener on the terms of the listener's emotional reaction to the behavior is a different proposition!

Consider my role as a negotiator in a lengthy conversation with a person contemplating violence. The impact of the "I"-Message is that for all this time I, the master listener, have been empathetically seeking to know more about the speaker's situation, emotions, and perception. I've asked open-ended questions, dropped minimal encouragers, reflected, and labeled every emotion she had. Now and for a fleeting moment, I am going to reveal my emotion and tie it to her actions. When I use it in the real world, it is a shock!

This technique, more than any of the other 8, quickly loses power if it is overused. The reason it is so effective is it functions like a psychological slap in the face. Too many slaps in the face and the novelty wears off, and the storyteller loses trust. Talk about your own emotions too much, and you are not being empathetic.

Don't forget to give the last part of the "I"-Message formula with the reason the behavior and the emotion are connected. The reason can be fairly vague. Use the word "because"! It is a powerfully persuasive word. The rational brain and the emotional brain like to hear it. It is a great preface to developing a theme. The theme is that the listener and speaker are on the "same team". Create this perception and a surrender is at hand.

The most common mistake I made when I first learned this listening tactic was to over-emphasis use of the "I"-Message with bad behavior. With over a decade of experience as an active listener now, I realize that "I"-Messages are best suited for encouraging and rewarding good decisions and actions. Anytime the speaker or person in crisis begins to seek our input for problem-solving, why not say, "I feel hopeful when you start asking about your options, because it means you'll make a better decision!" There are often more opportunities to use "I"-Messages to reward good behavior, and they generate more rapport than calling out bad behavior.

There are often more opportunities for the good behavior "I"-Messages and they generate more rapport than calling out bad behavior.

I have a modest proposal if you hold a position of authority in a company, non-profit, or are a parent. Make a commitment to use "I"-Messages every day to compliment and encourage. Create an atmosphere of positive reinforcement, and you are already a leader or parent who listens and cultivates powerful culture at work and at home!

If someone makes it personal, gets aggressive, or makes a threat, give them an "I"-Message. When they turn back towards consensus and logic and collaboration, give them an "I"-Message. Once they know you are listening to them, the "I"-Messages are in play. Use them!

❅ ❅ ❅

ALS NAME:
"I"-Messages

DEFINITION:
Rewarding and punishing your storyteller's behavior by sharing your emotion connected to that behavior with a reason.

USES:
Put a boundary around bad behavior;
Encourage good behavior;
Build rapport.

LIMITATIONS:
Riskiest technique when used to manage negative behavior. Requires that they care about your emotional state. Best used after

a period of intentional listening, emotion labeling, and good dialogue. Reserve the negative use (for bad behavior) for significant problems. Use the rewarding method for good behavior as often as you can without talking about yourself too much. MUST BE FORMULATED CORRECTLY! I feel (your emotion) when you (behavior), because (any sort of reason). Be concise. Don't emphasize their behavior, emphasize your emotion.

EXAMPLE(S):
Storyteller: "Maybe I should punch Steve in the face!"
Master Listener: "I feel sad when you talk about punching someone because I thought we were working together for a peaceful solution."

Storyteller: "I promise I won't punch Steve, even though I want to."
Master Listener: "I feel hopeful when you promise to not punch anyone because I know we can work together."

22. BUILDING A LISTENING CULTURE

a team that listens

"None of us, including me, ever do great things. But we can all do small things, with great love, and together we can do something wonderful." —Mother Teresa of Calcutta

There they are. You now have everything you need to master the eight active listening skills! Now, you can start putting them into play. The techniques are not designed to be kept in a drawer somewhere until needed. Although some clients have asked me for a list of the eight ALS techniques on a pocket card, that will not work. You cannot pull out the card in a crisis and begin rattling off the techniques when the goal is authentic empathy and trust.

These techniques are best suited to help us practice. When we supply the right attitude and motivation, they will make us naturally better at the nearly lost art of listening well. Negotiators use this system of eight skills to become well-rounded in their listening skill-set. During practice in our hostage negotiation unit, we use a scorecard to show negotiators which of the skills they are using well, which they are stumbling over, and which techniques they failed to utilize. I've found that if one technique is not resonating with a person in crisis, three others will. That's the beauty of this system.

Now that you are on your way to developing masterful listening habits, we should mention how futile it will be to do it alone! To become a master listener, you're going to need a community of like-minded listeners. Getting excited about a new skill or a new way of improving the skill is lovely. Without friends, that excitement fades quickly. Having a team who are also dedicated to becoming better listeners is invaluable. When they have the same foundation of terms and concepts, these partners can do amazing things in an organization. Without the team, the cacophony of the digital age will swallow each of them up.

Recall *Chapter 9: The Culture Beast*. Culture is a compelling aspect of human society and the organizations to which you belong. I regularly meet audience members at keynotes and students in my workshop who burn with desire to radically change their corporate culture. They complain of listening deficits, leaders who are awful listeners, and a complete lack of campfires! They ask me how they can transform their work culture or their direct supervisor. I smile.

In those moments, I remember the words of Mother Teresa that start this chapter. Or Leo Tolstoy when he penned these words, "Everyone thinks of changing the world, but no one thinks of changing himself." You don't control your culture. You don't control your boss! That is why thinking and listening like a hostage negotiator is the best way forward.

When I am bargaining for a life, I am never in control of the suspect's cultural influences! I just know about empathy, rapport, influence, and the active listening skills. I can only work daily to become the best listener and influencer possible. If I want to change people's minds, I change myself first. I do this before I even know who I want to influence. If you want to change your company or boss, change yourself.

Maybe you *are* the boss. If you are the CEO or president, you have incredible authority in the organization. You also have precisely the same level of control as everyone else reading this book when it comes to culture. You can't make culture do anything that "it" doesn't want. It is like a semi-inflated balloon that resists the push of your fist. It is resilient and flexible. Even the big boss has a boss. Whether a spouse, stakeholders, or a Board of Directors-everyone has someone they have to work with as a peer or subordinate. Thus, even the boss should proceed with a negotiator's mindset. If you want to change culture or bosses, you need to listen and negotiate.

Your culture, no matter how bad or good it is, needs you to be a better leader. The worst way to attempt to be a better leader is to try to generally lead better. This sentiment is the cause of a lot of ill-advised motivational talks, micro-management, unnecessary purchases of leadership books and seminar packages, and confusion at work.

I do not think you can become a better leader in any sort of work culture unless you improve your mastery of constituent skills: listening, negotiating, cultivation of culture, strategic planning, and problem-solving. Instead of being a better leader, become a better listener and focus on your culture!

Leading a culture is a special application of leadership. It is a risky activity. Mastery of cultural leadership means listening well to model this skill to everyone in the culture and to foster consensus about who the team is and what they ought to do.

I believe that leadership is not a skill. It is a craft.
A craft entails mastering supporting skills.

The power of incremental improvement in any one of the leadership skills elevates leadership across the board. Thus, by becoming a better listener one becomes a better negotiator. By negotiating well, problem-solving is made simple. Each skill has a relationship with the others. As a cohesive group, they form the nucleus of my speeches and workshops.

Eventually, I hope you will be granted the good fortune to discover and hone each of these skills. This book focuses on the first and foremost leadership skill in my experience. Master this skill and the rest become easier. Excel in this first skill and see the greatest increase in your success as a cultural leader. Listening is that skill.

Your company is not a person, but it behaves *like a person.* In this analogy, culture is its personality! Understanding your culture is now your job. To get to know your company's personality and to know the culture like you know the people, you'll need to use all of the listening skills I have given you. As many have handed them down to me, I hand them to you. Use them to accomplish four culture minding tasks:

1. Take the temperature
2. Flip the "saboteurs"
3. Feed the "gurus"
4. Manage perception

Take the temperature

If culture is informal and defies the best efforts of our control, how do we manage it? You need to take the temperature. Give your culture a wellness check! This may prove easier said than done. There is not an easy button for culture. There is no single point of access. The best method of determining the health and cultural personality of your firm is through longitudinal listening sessions with key people. Refer to *Chapter 9: The Culture Beast* for more ideas here. Intentional listening, practiced over time, builds the relationships you will need to begin the process of understanding your culture.

You must intentionally nurture ongoing conversations with your direct supervisor, peers, team, external partners, and clients. Use the active listening skills to develop relationships of trust where everyone is sitting at the culture campfire! Let them tell the truth about how things are. This is how we start to take the temperature. If something is ailing the culture, we will need to go deeper.

Flip the saboteurs

Now, let's flip over some flat rocks. It is possible you have negative influencers at work in your company's culture! These disgruntled, disenchanted and disengaged folks are ready to block necessary changes in the workplace. They climb on the backs of your hardest workers and snipe the innovators. I call them saboteurs. They are like J.R.R. Tolkien's goblins and orcs from *The Lord of the Rings*: never building and always burning. Left unhindered, they have a powerful influence on everyone else in your corporate culture.

This is not the sort of behavior you want spreading around. The saboteur is the employee that patiently waits for you to sell your change initiative or big project. Even though you ask for critiques or suggestions, they say nothing. As soon as you leave the room, the sabotage begins. "We tried that 10 years ago, and it will never work!" Behind your back, the saboteur plies his dark craft.

Before you get in a hurry to find them, consider what you should do once you succeed! Do not punish them. Listen to them! Bad emotional experiences create saboteurs in our business cultures. I have often Sometimes the saboteur is your owner. They are afraid to make the tough calls regarding culture. Once bitten, twice shy.

You have two choices to heal your culture of a saboteur. One option is to fire them. This might become necessary. For the good of the team and culture, you may have to cut out the cancer. That is less than ideal. The better option is to "flip" a saboteur. In my experience, saboteurs become masters of culture. They hide in the culture and learn to do the bare minimum to avoid detection and unwanted attention. These sort of skills and information networks can be invaluable to you as a cultural leader.

> *In my experience, saboteurs become masters of culture. They hide in the culture and learn to do the bare minimum to avoid detection and unwanted attention.*

This is the true test of listening. You will have to use all your skill to repair a relationship with someone your firm hired as a perfect fit and who has drifted away from the corporate mission. There is an uncanny parallel to my jumper. You must bring this talented employee back from the edge through persuasion. The decision to flip or be fired is theirs. If you can convince them to speak candidly with you about their needs and perspectives on the organization, you might convert them to become something very different: a positive cultural influence.

Feed the gurus

Here's a critical exercise for you to build better cultural health in your organization. Identify the positive influencers and feed them with more authority and resources to accomplish their work. At every level of authority in your firm, there are influencers. For now, focus on these crucial influencers. If you don't know who they are, then you are missing out on a fantastic source of information about the health and future of your company. I like to call them gurus.

When people need answers, advice, or guidance, they go to the gurus. Authority does not automatically make you a guru. They are not in the employee manual. They are a cultural feature. Gurus help move the right people and the right ideas to the right places in any organization. Gurus are proof of the power of influence and culture. Reward them, encourage them, and ask them to do more.

> *When people need answers, advice, or*
> *guidance they go to the gurus. Authority*
> *does not automatically make you a guru.*

Manage perception

A critical feature of culture is perception. Within the culture, every single person has some understanding of core concepts and values the organization has deemed vital. Not all these understandings are the same. The larger the organization, the more likely that some of the people inside of it have conflicting perceptions of these things.

Taming the culture beast means conducting an alignment of perception. Perception in the listening realm refers to our ability to understand based on our experience. What we have learned to this point in our lives heavily influences how we see the world. This extends to the messages our leaders give us. It can be as simple as giraffes!

I use a picture of two giraffes in my seminars to illustrate the power of perception. Two giraffes facing each other with necks crossed in an embrace can appear to the uninitiated to be a sign of affection. Usually, only a few of my students correctly state that this is how giraffes fight. Why do we see a hug when giraffes, zoologists, and Animal Planet junkies see violence and aggression? Because, we rely upon our experiences to interpret our environment. In our experience, placing my neck against another person's neck is perceived as loving and trusting due to the vulnerability of this action. We haven't aligned our perception with zoological knowledge!

As a police officer, I see the world differently than non-police officers. Out in public, I drive my wife crazy with my observation and analysis of human behavior indicating defensiveness, anxiety and deception, and physiological signs of drug use. My brother-in-law, who raises registered Angus cattle, can spot signs of trouble in the herd long before a city-slicker. This specialized knowledge comes from experience, whether we are talking about hostage-takers or heifers.

Listeners must learn to expand their perception. Great leaders and lovers become masters of understanding their audience and choosing appeals and language designed to fit their colleagues' perceptions. Over the course of time, you can become adept at changing your vocabulary, posture, and even para-verbal patterns to meet the perception level of whomever you wish to persuade.

Great leaders and lovers become masters of understanding their audience and choosing appeals and language designed to fit their colleagues' perceptions.

Leaders are the keepers of culture. They do well to place a high value on listening and consensus building in their culture at work. They understand that people crave culture. We need the community of like-minded folk. We need a tribe. We want guidance beyond the regulation manual. We want to belong.

The image of a ferocious beast is appropriate for your workplace culture. It, like all organic things, is constantly changing. It's alive and adapting. It is a living, breathing creature. Its health waxes and wanes as it is cultivated or allowed to go feral. Leaders make their salary taming the culture beast by focusing on building a culture of intentional listening where campfires are breaking out all the time.

Go out and listen to your people. Fight culture with culture. Teach your key employees how to give and receive criticism. Build up influencers to counteract sabotage. Ask them who they can trust for honest advice. Watch and learn who mentors and sacrifices with no promise of return. Watch for the chuckleheads who are cutting telegraph wires, burning bridges, and ripping up the railroads! Bring them back to the tribe as gurus through the proven process of empathetic listening, rapport building, and influence. If that doesn't work, vote them off your cultural island.

Managing culture is closely tied to listening well. If you are working in a culture that has not placed a high value on intentional listening, you are in for a painful journey. Culture tends to attract or repel members based on their affinity for cultural features. A poor listening culture attracts poor listeners and it gets worse. A listening culture attracts master listeners and gets better. The glue of this sort of golden corporate culture is empathetic understanding. Imagine the power if 10% of your key people, gurus and their like, made a serious commitment to the sort of listening described in this book and held each other to account as they became master listeners.

Here's how to make intentional, authentic, and effective listening a feature of your culture at work or home. Provide a common foundation of language to describe this ideal way to listen. Incorporate skills-based cultural learning of listening techniques. Challenge each other and hold each other accountable in the manner I describe in this book. As every member of the cultural body improves their listening, the culture thrives.

23. THE HOMEFRONT

listen to your family first

Upon being questioned about how to promote world peace:
"Go home and love your family."   —*Mother*
Teresa of Calcutta

Presidents and CEOs hire me to train their key personnel in listening and negotiating skills. Trade shows and professional associations hire me to entertain their conference audiences all the time. These captains of industry value the principles of cultural leadership and listening that you've read in this book. Whether for sales and marketing, organizational development, or productivity gains, my clients always find value in these events. Now, I must make a confession! Despite the clear application of authentic listening to the business world, I do not think that making money is the best use of active listening, empathy, and rapport.

Families are the most important cultures. I am a husband to my wonderful wife and father to our six adopted children. If authentic listening culture is important enough to cultivate on our police negotiation team, serving felons and people with mental illness, I am a fool if I don't practice what I preach in my own home for my kiddos. Our children and family members have a story to tell, just like everyone at work.

Families are the bedrock of civilization. This bedrock has been shaken. As goes the institution of the modern family, so goes our society and nation. Our rates of divorce, abuse, neglect, and psychological trauma indicate a poverty not measured in dollars and cents. What is missing is love in the form of high-fidelity listening habits.

For you to accelerate towards masterful listening, it cannot be a 9-to-5 act in the office. It cannot be a sales gimmick. Listening must begin and end at home and become a natural response to the needs of every human person you encounter! Our relationships must be built upon authentic listening, and it must come from our deepest habitude.

I intend for you to have the best listening habits with your family in your home, no matter how big your family happens to be. Naturally, listen to your 11 children! If you are single with no kids and no plans to change that, I pray just as hard that you nurture meaningful relationships away from the workplace. They must be rooted in genuine listening. Even as just a single person, you might be the nucleus of something bigger- a family of friends or like-minded thinkers. History is full of examples of friendships and ensembles, the Inklings come to mind, who strive for a stronger civil society. Listening is still the key ingredient to building a strong sense of community.

If you commit any portion of this short book to memory, let it be that listening is best when it is a service to the most vulnerable. Listening to children is perhaps the grandest enrichment you will achieve through intentional listening. Their sense of innocence and wonder is perfect for warming your soul. It will test the effectiveness of the active listening skills you employ. Empathy and rapport are right and just to extend to toddlers, tweens, and, yes, even teenagers.

---

*...listening is best when it is a service
to the most vulnerable.*

Once my children were speaking sentences, employing most of the active listening skills was possible. Our kids are adept at pushing our buttons, and their comfort with our speaking and communication habits make them a particularly instructive listening partner. If your kids are often getting emotional reactions from you, it's time to listen deeply to what they are trying to tell you by being attentive and responding appropriately!

Take my 12-year-old daughter, Trinity. She is an introvert. Trinity is a challenging listening partner after school! I, like most parents, could ask, "Did you have a good day at school?" That is a closed-ended question! An open-ended question like "How was your day at school?" is preferred. What might be better is this: "Tell me about school today!" Sell it with an energetic and empathetic tone, and it might just get more than a grunt in response! Now try this: "Tell me about the best thing that happened at school today!" with a follow-up, "Tell me about the worst thing that happened at school today." These are open-ended too, but more likely to get a response in my experience. We are not done yet!

There is an even better way to ask Trinity for her story today. The active listening skills complement each other. A paraphrase or an emotion label with an open-ended question is the sort of inquiry that moves tweens to answer. Try, "You look exhausted..." or "I know school can be tough right now..." plus "...tell me about your school day!"

The last use of great questioning is the "What if" technique. "What if you didn't have to go to school today? What would you have done instead? Where would you go? With whom? Why?" The only limit to the effectiveness of well-made questions is our imagination. For the same reason you listen to kids, seek out the lonely people on the edge of your life. The poor, the ill, and those who struggle with addiction and mental illness all have stories too.

The sort of listening I endorse is not a sales gimmick. It's not a parlor trick. If it were, then I would be angry if you tried them on your spouse! The beauty of listening well and using these proven techniques is that even when another person knows what you are about, they still love you for the effort.

The sort of listening I endorse is not a sales gimmick. It's not a parlor trick.

My wife has seen all my keynotes and trainings over the years. She has watched me in my journey from beat cop to negotiator to negotiations commander. She knows the active listening skills! Sometimes when we have a marital disagreement, I'll naturally begin to label emotions or paraphrase her concerns. She responds quickly- "Don't use that negotiator stuff on me!" They still work. These techniques are still effective for her and help defuse an emotional conversation. She appreciates the results even when she recognizes the methods. The members of my negotiation team use the techniques to listen better to each other. We don't resent these methods. We recognize that our colleague cares.

Leadership and love are the two core activities that listening supports best. Your family and mine both desperately need leaders and lovers. Listening is not a business model. It is a way of life! It belongs in your home.

24. AN ENDING THAT IS A BEGINNING

you are sent

"It's hard to beat a person who doesn't give up."
—George Herman "Babe" Ruth Jr.

re you wondering what happened to my friend, the parking garage jumper? Despite my initial failures, my fear of saying the wrong thing, and my mistaken belief that the decision to jump was in any part mine, I eventually struck it rich out of desperation. When I ran out of emotional energy and ineffective pleadings, I finally gave in and asked, "Why are we here?" She told me her story. Her uncle jumped from this roof a few years ago on this very date. She was having relationship problems and no one in her family cared. She struggled with addiction. I asked more questions, and she told me more about why she wanted to jump. Then she told me why she didn't want to jump. After about an hour, she told me, "I think you are trying to listen." She climbed over the guardrail and went to the hospital with me.

On the top deck of the six-story parking garage, I had gotten a taste of crisis negotiation. I wanted to learn more. Eight years after my six-story adventure, I became a hostage negotiator. I

LIFE OR DEATH LISTENING

trained with the FBI and many other experienced local and State law enforcement professionals engaged in this craft of ours all over the nation and world. I became a seasoned negotiator on an active SWAT team.

Now, here is the epilogue to the parking garage. Ten years later, I was working a midnight shift. A patrol sergeant called me on my cell phone and asked for my help. He needed a negotiator. I drove across town with lights flashing and siren wailing. I climbed a cloverleaf interchange in the center of our city, where a northbound to westbound ramp arches high over the entire interstate highway. A woman was straddling the guardrail. A bunch of police officers was staring at her from the base of the ramp. With my first jumper, I didn't have time to think. I had no plan. This time was different. I was rehearsing in my mind the skills and techniques I have come to rely upon after hundreds of street-level encounters and many high stakes negotiations for the SWAT team. I was armed with experience and confidence in my craft.

I walked cautiously up the ramp. I used her first name. I let her lead. I listened to the woman and practiced active listening to gain her trust. I asked the right questions to learn early on why she wanted to die. Her baby boy had died. She was distraught and suffering from post-partum depression. She hurt so badly and wanted to be with her recently deceased infant son.

One hour later, after some tough questions from her and some serious listening from me, she asked what she should do. A few minutes later, a patrol officer and I were patiently waiting for her at the cemetery as she spent some time at her son's grave. A few minutes after that, she and I walked into a local hospital for her to get the help she needed.

The two women and their stories have some similarities. Both the women were depressed and suicidal. Both were convinced that the pain they felt from loss could be ended along with their own life. Both chose lethal heights. Both had something holding them here with the living. I had two different experiences working with each. The difference for me on the overpass was the education of the parking garage. I firmly held the commitment to intentional listening and the understanding that the decision to jump was not mine. Leading her meant listening to her. As a rookie cop, I proposed to myself that if I wanted to become a master listener, I would have to study from the best and put in the hard work. I did. I honed my listening skill without knowing that one decade later it would all be put to the test again.

As a rookie cop, I proposed to myself that if I wanted to become a master listener, I would have to study from the best and put in the hard work.

Now my friend, this great proposal is yours. If you feel compelled to lead and love better by listening well, then use this book and its simple message to do just that. Listening is life. Go live it. Here's how.

If you read the first few chapters and immediately thought, "I need to be a better listener!", then you are thinking rightly. If you also were overwhelmed by the thought of beginning this long and difficult journey towards mastering listening, you are not alone.

The King of Hearts in Lewis Carroll's nonsense story, *Alice in Wonderland*, said it best. "Begin at the beginning," the King said, very gravely, "and go on till you come to the end; then stop."

Begin right now. Start by taking stock of what you have in the way of listening skills. Take the quiz in *Chapter 6: Not Listening* and prioritize the bad listening habits you may have. Now get feedback! Go have a direct, intensive conversation with your boss, your direct reports, and as many trusted colleagues as you can. Ask them what they think of your listening skills. Ask them what your reputation as a leader and listener is within the organization. Sell to them your sincerity in receiving an honest appraisal. Commission these same people. Describe your goals as a student of listening. Name the bad habit you are trying to eliminate and ask them to help you in correcting this behavior. Every time you slip up, name the habit and then embrace this fraternal correction!

Listening intentionally is for leaders. Listening authentically is for lovers. It is excellence in the workplace managing teams. It is the only way I know to love your family. No matter who you are, where you are, what you do, or how good you already are, you can get better. How good do you want to be? Now go do it! The only way you will fail is if you quit. There will be mistakes and missteps. I should know. I have failed in listening opportunities many times in the last decade. I am a much better listener for those failures. Take courage and follow me!

In the year 2000, I found myself in an assembly of young men in the basement of a Roman Catholic seminary. I was just a young man discerning a call to the priesthood. The rector that evening, the first day of the semester, said something to us that has stuck with me for my whole life. "You are all here for the wrong reason." This was a disturbing statement. It is unfortunate that I must apply it to you, my dear reader. The meaning of the rector's startling remark was that he cared less about the why of our arriving and more about what we would be doing now that we were there. In a similar way, I don't care why you found this book and read all the way to the last page. I care much more what you do with this opportunity to become a great listener. Here and now- a wonderful place and time to begin for the good of your work culture or culture at home.

It is time to depart on this journey to become a master listener. You are sent.

QUICK REFERENCE

field guides for master listeners

THE 8 ACTIVE LISTENING SKILLS

1. OPEN-ENDED QUESTIONS
2. MINIMAL ENCOURAGERS
3. REFLECTING
4. EMOTION LABELING
5. EFFECTIVE PAUSES
6. PARAPHRASING
7. SUMMARIZING
8. "I"-MESSAGES

LIFE OR DEATH LISTENING
by DAN OBLINGER

LISTENING SKILLS
IMPROVEMENT PLAN

THE BAD LISTENING HABIT I AM REDUCING:

_____

- Name it.
- Recognize it before it happens or at least after.
- Self-correct.
- Commission your trusted people to hold you accountable.
- Thank them for correcting you.

THE NEW ACTIVE LISTENING SKILL TO MASTER:

_____

- Read the chapter again for this skill.
- Practice, practice, practice!
- Look for at least one opportunity at work, at home,

and in public with a stranger to use this ALS technique today.

- Commission your trusted people to hold you accountable.
- Thank them for correcting you.

ONLY ONE OF EACH AT A TIME! WHEN YOU RECOGNIZE IMPROVEMENT, SWITCH TO THE NEXT HABIT/SKILL.

COMMONLY LABELED EMOTIONS

"It seems/looks/sounds like you are…"

POSITIVE	PROBLEMATIC	SAFE
Content	Worried	Concerned
Happy	Dejected	Sad
Grateful	Ungrateful	Let down
Supported	Isolated	Lonely
	"Pissed Off"	Angry
Hopeful	Hopeless	Out of options
Joyful	Depressed	Down
Ambitious	Helpless	Confused
Ecstatic	Vengeful	Wronged
Satisfied	Anxious	
Peaceful		Grieving

CUSTOMER SERVICE SHORT CUT
Disappointed, Frustrated, and Disgusted

NOW WHAT?

Since you bought this book or an amazing friend gifted it to you, I want to extend to you an offer. Use what it contains. Make a plan to improve your listening. Be bold! Take risks. When your listening ambition outpaces your current listening skill, contact me! Tell me what happened and let's have a conversation. If you succeed wildly, I would love to hear that too. For either event, reach me at dan.oblinger@gmail.com or on LinkedIn. If you would like to see more about listening and ALS, check out my Youtube channel at "Dan Oblinger Speaks" or at www.masterlistener.com.

Please consider writing a positive review at Amazon.com. Your feedback is critical to spreading my message promoting the importance of listening skills and how to start making them better for the sake of families, communities, and corporations!

My second book is entitled The 28 Laws of Listening. It offers additional lessons in masterful listening and a 28 days program of structured activities to build a wonderful habit of listening authentically. I highly recommend it now that you have read this work.

My final word on listening is that there is certainly more to leadership and caring for others. I think listening is the foundation of all good things when it comes to relationships with human beings. Negotiating, problem solving, strategic planning are also important skills that are distinct from listening and worthy of your study. Listening serves them all. It makes all those other activities more valuable. Listening itself is a valuable service to human beings and opens up opportunities for other forms of team-building, consensus, and cooperation. Even when others won't listen or refuse to participate in good faith, listening is a powerful gift you offer. Even when the gift is not accepted, the gesture is powerful and is nearly always reciprocated somehow. Listen until it hurts! You won't be disappointed.

ABOUT THE AUTHOR

Dan Oblinger

Dan Oblinger is a unique voice in corporate training and keynotes. He is a father, husband, philosopher, and lawman. Oblinger has been successful in his professional life as a hostage negotiator, undercover human trafficking investigator, chicken rancher, drug recognition expert, human resources consultant, ditch digger, landlord, grocery bagger, onion ring maker, small business owner, and beat cop.

Dan's habit of culture management as the commander of several elite units of investigators and negotiators informs his belief in what he teaches. He has used his unique experiences and high energy humor to educate audiences across America since 2008. Dan has carved out a niche as a leading expert in providing speaking, training, and executive consulting for diverse industries and client firms. Dan's passion is sharing listening, negotiating, and leadership skills so everyone can become more authentic leaders and lovers. His message is simple and refreshing: Listen well and negotiate for consensus to cultivate excellence in corporate culture. Dan currently builds internal teams of negotiators and active listening practitioners for his corporate clients, predominantly civil engineering firms.

Everyone has an amazing story to tell, and it is our job to invite them to tell it! Dan lives happily with his wife, six adopted children, and flock of chickens on a small homestead in rural Kansas. Ad Astra Per Aspera!

Want to have him speak at your conference or train your key people? Make your inquiry at www.masterlistener.com.

BOOKS BY THIS AUTHOR

The 28 Laws Of Listening:

This is a 4-week guided tour of best practices in listening well. If you loved Life or Death Listening and want to begin to build habits of excellence in active listening, The 28 Laws of Listening represents the ultimate guide! It focuses on the methods and mindset necessary to foster a culture of authentic listening and trust. The author relates lessons learned in two decades of police work and hostage negotiation and another decade of corporate training and keynoting. It represents the absolute cutting edge of theory and practice for active listening practitioners and negotiators.

Each law has a corresponding challenge designed for the reader to put the lesson into action to build good listening habits.

Printed in Great Britain
by Amazon

33297738R00088